Disclaimer

This book is intended to provide accurate information for personal, educational, and entertainment purposes. It is not meant to offer legal, financial, medical, or other professional advice. While the author and publisher have made every effort to ensure the information is correct and up to date, they make no guarantees regarding its accuracy, completeness, or suitability for any purpose.

The author and publisher disclaim any liability for any direct or indirect losses or damages resulting from the use or misuse of the information provided in this book. Readers are encouraged to seek professional advice when needed. The author and publisher are not responsible for any consequences, including but not limited to errors, omissions, or any damages incurred as a result of following the strategies or information in this book.

CONTENTS

Author Info

Dianne Williams developed a strong understanding of money management early, opening her first savings account at age ten with encouragement from her parents. This sparked her interest in financial planning. As a teen, she worked as a checkout operator, learning valuable lessons in time management and customer service. After high school, she pursued both arts and accounting in college, blending creativity with financial skills.

As a teacher, Dianne has inspired students in both arts and finance, and she is known for her engaging and practical teaching methods. Fascinated by technology, she was always willing to embrace digital advancements in her work. Now semi-retired, she enjoys hobbies like art, photography, and travel while still continuing to help others. Dianne credits her parents for instilling lifelong values of hard work and financial responsibility, which she now shares with the next generation through teaching and writing.

Note To Parents And Teachers

Parents and teachers have an important role in helping kids learn about money. By teaching your children and students how to manage money, you can help set them up for a secure future. Talking often about saving, spending, and budgeting makes these topics easier for teens to understand. Your help now can lead to good habits that will benefit them for the rest of their lives.

You can make lessons more interesting by talking about current events, like digital currencies, changes in the economy, or other money-related news. When teens can relate lessons to real-world situations, it makes learning much more meaningful. Doing activities together can also make learning more fun and help you bond with your teen. Setting goals and celebrating when they reach them will help boost their confidence and make them feel more motivated.

It's important to offer advice but also let them make their own choices. This helps kids become independent while still knowing they have your support. Encourage your teens to try real-life experiences, like making a budget or earning money by babysitting, mowing lawns, or pet sitting. These activities teach the value of earning money and help them appreciate it. There are also many apps that can make this more accessible and interesting for young people. Share your own money experiences and talk about real situations to make the learning more relatable.

Teach them how to use basic tools like budget planners, spreadsheets, or apps to manage their money. Talk about the difference between needs and wants to help them make smart spending decisions. Empower kids to see through the smoke and mirrors of advertising.

Help them understand how these messages can influence their spending, and show them how to recognize these sneaky tactics so they can make better choices. Inform kids about the risks and rewards of money decisions and the value of giving back to the community, which helps build empathy and social responsibility. Show them why it's important to budget, save for the future, and avoid unnecessary debt.

Make talking about money a regular part of your family life - whether it's around the dinner table or at specific times set aside for these discussions. As a teacher, incorporate these conversations into your daily classroom life. Effective money management is one of the most important things that kids will ever need to learn, so taking an interdisciplinary approach is a great way to demonstrate that importance. These conversations should happen in every type of classroom, not just financial math or economics.

Consistent conversations help keep money topics fresh in their minds and show them why good financial habits are important. Tailor your approach to what works best for your teen—some may like hands-on activities, while others might prefer reading or talking. Tune in to their learning styles, and be flexible to help keep them interested. Celebrate their progress, even the small wins, to keep them motivated and reinforce good habits.

You can help kids build a strong foundation for financial independence and success. Learning about money is something that continues throughout life, and your guidance will make a big difference. By staying involved and encouraging teens to explore, you are preparing them to handle money challenges with confidence. The support you give them today will provide skills that will benefit them for the rest of their lives and set them up for a secure future.

When they are ready, introduce more advanced topics, like credit scores, interest rates, and investments. Start in a simple way and build from there. These ideas may seem complicated, but learning about them early can make them easier to understand later on. Using resources like articles, videos, or workshops is a great way to help deepen their understanding.

Encourage your teen to take on small projects, like saving for something they want or planning a budget for an event. These real-life projects make learning about money more meaningful and help them remember important concepts. The more they connect financial lessons to their everyday life, the better they will understand them. Additionally, these types of activities can be a huge motivator and confidence booster for a young person.

Your role as a parent or teacher is crucial. By being interested in their financial education, you are helping to build a strong foundation for their success. With your guidance, encouragement, and shared learning experiences, you can help kids and teens develop a positive attitude about money that will benefit them throughout their lives.

INTRODUCTION

MONEY IS A HUGE part of everyday life. Whether buying lunch at school, saving up for a new game, or thinking about college, money plays a big role. Many teens wonder how to make their allowance last, or how to save for something special. Understanding the "how" of managing money can help you make good choices now and in the future. And the better those choices are that you make right now, the better off you will be in the future.

You might have questions like: How can I save money? What's the best way to budget? How do banks work? Learning about these topics can seem hard, but it doesn't have to be. By building money skills, you can feel more in control. Think about being able to save for things you want and still have money left over. Having good money habits can make your life easier.

Some teens feel stressed about money because they don't understand how it works. By learning now, you will avoid problems later. Knowing how to budget can help you effectively plan your spending. Understanding how banking works can show you how to keep your money safe. Learning about different ways to earn money can empower you with more options. You might even discover new interests, like investing or starting a small business.

Your path to money mastery can start with simple steps. By working through activities, you can practice what you have learned. Hands-on tasks make learning fun and memorable. You might work on creating a budget, setting savings goals, or exploring how interest works. These activities help you apply concepts to real-life situations.

Some topics might seem challenging at first, but with practice, they will become easier. The QR codes provided here can give you extra resources if you want to learn more. By scanning a code, you can access tools or detailed explanations. This can help you stay current with the latest information. Technology does wonders for making learning more interactive and engaging.

You can explore topics like digital banking or cryptocurrency. Bitcoin might be a new concept for you, but it's becoming more important than ever in today's world. Understanding different types of money can broaden your knowledge about how to make and use money. As you learn, be encouraged to start thinking about your own financial goals. Setting goals gives you something to work toward.

Whether it's saving for a car, college, or a trip, having solid money skills will help you get there. Good habits now leads to success later. Managing money is a skill that can benefit you throughout your life. You don't have to feel overwhelmed by money matters. Breaking down topics into simple steps can make them easier to understand.

You might find that you enjoy learning about finance. Sharing what you learn with friends can be fun, too. It's a great way to form community around building good money habits, and teaching others reinforces your own learning. Together, you and your friends can support each other in reaching your goals. It's okay to ask questions and seek help when needed. No one expects you to know everything right away. Learning is a process that takes time and effort.

With each new topic, you build on what you've learned before. Patience and practice will lead you to mastery. Think of money skills as tools you can use in many areas of life. They can help you make informed decisions. Having a good understanding of money can give you confidence. You might feel more prepared for the challenges that come your way.

By taking charge of your finances, you can shape your future. The choices you make now can have a big impact later on. So why not start learning today? You have the ability to succeed in managing your money. Just take it one step at a time, and don't be afraid to explore new topics. The more you learn, the more options you may have.

Money mastery isn't about being perfect; it's about making progress. Make sure to celebrate your achievements along the way. Every small step counts toward your goals! Stay curious and keep an open mind. You never know where your new skills might lead you. Perhaps you'll start a business, invest, or help others with their finances.

The possibilities are endless when you have the right tools. Take the opportunity to learn and grow. Your future self will thank you for the effort you put in now. Money doesn't have to be a mystery. By understanding it, you can make it work for you. Knowledge is power, and in this case, it can lead to financial freedom.

Start today, and see how far you can go. Some teens start small businesses like mowing lawns or selling crafts. Understanding money better can help you more effectively manage earnings from jobs like babysitting or tutoring. You might use what you learn to budget for school supplies or hobbies. Knowing how to save can help you reach your goals faster.

Money skills can also help you avoid debt in the future. By making smart choices now, you can keep your finances healthy. It's never too early to start learning about money. Even small steps can make a big difference over time. You might be surprised at how much you can save just by making a plan.

Money management is a valuable life skill - arguably one of the most valuable life skills there is. Think of it this way: mastering financial skills isn't just about dollars and cents; it is about building confidence that can transform your life. Money skills have a ripple effect and can help you in many areas, including decision-making and planning. Confidence in handling money can often spill over into other parts of your life. You may find that you feel more independent and capable. Friends and family might notice these positive changes, as well. And you can even inspire others.

CHAPTER 1

WHAT IS MONEY AND HOW TO GET IT

Forms of money from past to present

MONEY HAS BEEN AROUND for a very long time. People have always needed a way to trade things. Long ago, humans swapped items like shells, beads, or even cows. This was called bartering. If someone had extra grain but needed meat, they would find someone who had meat but needed grain.

Carrying goods to trade wasn't always easy. So, people started using metals like gold and silver. These metals were special because they were shiny and didn't rust. People made coins out of them. Coins were easier to carry than bags of grain or livestock.

Paper money came next. Instead of carrying heavy coins, people could carry lightweight paper notes. These notes stood for a certain amount of gold or silver kept in a safe place. This made buying and selling things much simpler.

In recent times, we have moved toward using electronic money. This includes credit cards, debit cards, and online banking. With just a swipe or a click, people can pay for things without using cash. This is handy because it is fast and you don't need to carry money around.

Today, there is even a new type of money called cryptocurrency. Bitcoin is the most famous one currently. It is digital money that exists only on computers. People use it to buy things online. It is different because it is not controlled by any government or bank.

In those early days, communities used items that were valuable to them as money. For example, in some places, salt was very valuable. People used salt to preserve food, so it was extremely important. Ancient peoples traded salt for other goods and services. In other areas, cacao beans were used as money, because they were the key ingredient in making chocolate.

The use of coins started in places like ancient Lydia, which is now part of Turkey. The first coins were made of a mix of gold and silver called electrum. Each coin had a stamp to show its value. This made it easier to know how much each coin was worth.

As trade between countries grew, so did the need for money that was accepted in many places. This led to the creation of standardized coins and later paper money. The Chinese were some of the first people to use paper money. They would write promises to pay on pieces of paper.

Paper money quickly spread to other parts of the world. Banks began to print banknotes. These notes were promises to pay the bearer a certain amount of gold or silver. This system was called "the gold standard." It meant that paper money could be exchanged for gold.

In the 20th century, many countries moved away from the gold standard. This meant that their money was no longer backed by gold. Instead, the value of money was based on trust in the government and the economy. This is called "fiat money."

With the rise of computers and the internet, electronic money became more common. People started using credit cards and debit cards. Online banking allowed people to move money without having to go to the bank. This made managing money much more convenient.

Cryptocurrencies like Bitcoin are the latest form of money. They use technology called "blockchain" to keep track of transactions. Many people find cryptocurrencies exciting because they are new and different. However, they can also be risky because their value can change rapidly.

Throughout history, money has always been about making trade easier. Each new form of money has tried to solve problems with the old forms. Coins were easier than barter. Paper money was lighter than coins. Electronic money is faster than cash. Cryptocurrencies offer new possibilities for the future.

Looking back at the history of money shows how it has evolved through the ages. This helps us understand how important money is in our lives. It also shows that money can and will change, and we need to be ready to learn about new forms of money.

Making/Earning money - income, interest, business, entrepreneurship

Earning money is something everyone needs to learn about. We all use money, and there are many ways to make money. Some people work a job and get paid a wage or salary. Others start their own businesses. Some earn money through investments.

When working for someone else, you usually get paid for your time and skills. This is called income. Jobs can be full-time or part-time. It's important to find work that you enjoy and that pays you fairly.

Starting your own business is another way to earn money. This is called entrepreneurship. Entrepreneurs come up with ideas for products or services. They take risks to start a company. If the business does well, they can earn a lot of money. Starting a business can be hard work, and can come with many risks, but it can also be very rewarding.

Interest is money you earn from lending your money to others. When you put money in a bank account, the bank uses your money to lend to others. In return, the bank pays you interest, which means your money can grow over time. Saving money in a bank is a safe way to earn interest.

Investing is when you put your money into something with the hope that it will grow. This could be stocks, bonds, or real estate. Investing can earn you more money than just saving. However, investing can also be risky. It's important to learn about investments before putting your money into them.

Creating something unique can also earn you money. This could be writing a book, making art, or inventing a new product. When people buy your creations, you earn money. If you have a special talent or skill, this can be an incredibly fulfilling way to earn.Earning money is not just about making as much as possible. It's also about doing something you enjoy. If you like your work, you will be happier. It's important to think about what you are good at and what you enjoy when choosing how you would like to earn money.

There are also many ways to earn money online. You can sell items on websites, do freelance work, or make videos, just to name a few. The internet has made it possible for people to earn money from anywhere.

No matter how you choose to earn money, smart management is key to unlocking your financial potential. This means building a nest egg for future adventures and spending with intention. Learning about budgeting can help you make the most of the money you earn.

Setting goals for yourself is useful. Think about what you want to achieve. Do you want to save for college? Do you want to buy a car? Having goals can help you stay motivated to achieve your desires.

Earning money takes time and effort. But with hard work and smart choices, you can earn steadily and reach your goals.

Setting Up an Online Store on Etsy

1. **Visit Etsy**: Open your web browser and go to www.etsy.com.
2. **Create an Account**: Click on "Sign in" at the top right corner, then select "Register" to sign up with your email.
3. **Confirm Your Email**: Check your inbox for a confirmation email from Etsy and click the link provided.
4. **Open Your Shop**: After logging in, click on "Sell on Etsy" and then "Get started" to begin setting up your shop.
5. **Set Shop Preferences**: Choose your shop language, country, and currency. Click "Save and continue."
6. **Name Your Shop**: Enter a unique name that reflects your products. Click "Save and continue."
7. **Stock Your Shop**: Click "Add a listing" to upload photos and details of the items you want to sell.
8. **Choose Payment Method**: Select how you wish to receive payments (e.g., Direct Checkout, PayPal).
9. **Set Up Billing**: Provide necessary billing information for seller fees.
10. **Launch Your Shop**: Review all details and click "Open your shop" to go live.
11. **Promote Your Shop**: Share your shop link on social media and with friends and family.

Taxation - a necessary evil for a healthy society

Taxes are money that people pay to the government. When you earn money, you might have to pay some of it in taxes. Taxes are used to pay for things that everyone needs, like schools, roads, and hospitals.

Some people don't like paying taxes. They might feel like they are losing money, but taxes help make our society better. Without taxes, we wouldn't have many of the services we need.

When you buy something at the store, you might pay sales tax - a small part of the price that goes to the government. Similarly, when you earn money from a job, you might pay income tax - a portion of your earnings that also goes to the government.

Additionally, businesses also pay taxes. They play their part by paying taxes on their profits. This helps make sure that everyone contributes to society as a whole.

Taxes are important because they fund public services which includes things like police and firefighters. Taxes also help pay for public places like parks and libraries. These are things that everyone can use.

Sometimes, taxes can be used to help people who are in need. This might include public programs that help people who are sick or who have lost their jobs.

It's important to understand how taxes work. When you start earning money, you might need to fill out tax forms. This can seem complicated, but there are people who can help.

Sometimes people try to avoid paying taxes. This is not a good idea. Not paying taxes can lead to trouble with the law. It's better to be honest and pay the taxes you owe to avoid any trouble down the line.

Paying taxes is a part of being a responsible citizen. It shows that you care about your community. By paying taxes, you help make sure that everyone has access to important services.

It's also good to learn about how taxes are used. This can help you understand why they are important and why they are considered a part of our civic duty. It can also help you make choices about voting and being involved in your community.

In some countries, taxes are higher than in others. This means that people pay more of their earnings to the government. In return, they might get more services, like free healthcare or college education.

Learning about how taxes work where you live will help you plan for the future. If you know how much you need to pay in taxes, you can budget your money better.

While paying taxes might not be fun, it helps make our society work. By contributing, we all help each other.

Learning About Taxes Using the IRS Website

1. **Visit the IRS Website: Go to www.irs.gov.**
2. **Navigate to 'Help & Resources'**: Hover over "Help & Resources" in the top menu.
3. **Select 'Teens' Page**: Click on "Tax Information for Students" under the "Students" section.
4. **Read Educational Materials**: Explore topics like "Why Pay Taxes?" and "Understanding Taxes."
5. **Access 'Understanding Taxes' Program**: Click on the link to the "Understanding Taxes" module.
6. **Choose 'Student Site'**: Select the "Student Site" option to access interactive lessons.
7. **Explore the Modules**: Navigate through modules covering tax history, laws, and simulations.
8. **Complete Interactive Activities**: Engage with activities to apply what you've learned.

9. **Take Quizzes**: Test your knowledge with quizzes provided in the lessons.
10. **Discuss with a Mentor**: Talk about what you've learned with a teacher or parent for deeper understanding.

Exercises:

1. **Money Evolution Timeline**: Create a timeline showing the evolution of money from bartering to cryptocurrency, including at least five key milestones.
2. **Income Exploration**: List three ways you can earn money as a teen and describe how each method generates income.
3. **Interest Calculation**: If you deposit $100 in a savings account with a 2% annual interest rate, calculate how much money you'll have after one year.
4. **Business Idea Brainstorm**: Think of a small business you could start. Outline the product or service and how you'd market it.
5. **Tax Benefits Research**: Identify three public services funded by taxes and explain why they are important to your community.
6. **Money Management Plan**: Write down five strategies to take control of your money instead of letting it control you.

Case Studies: Real Money Stories

Sarah's Street Tacos

Sarah always dreamed of running her own restaurant. Instead of taking a huge loan for a traditional restaurant, she started small with a food truck selling authentic Mexican street tacos. Initial investment: $15,000 from savings.

Key Decisions:

- Started small to test the market
- Used social media for free marketing

- Tracked daily sales meticulously
- Reinvested profits into equipment

Outcome: After two years, Sarah owns three food trucks and is planning her first brick-and-mortar restaurant. Her story shows how starting small and reinvesting profits can build a successful business.

Mike's Bitcoin Journey

Mike invested $1,000 in Bitcoin in 2020 without understanding cryptocurrency markets. When the price surged, excitement led him to invest another $5,000 at the peak.

What Went Wrong:

- No research before investing
- Invested based on emotions
- Put too much money in at once
- Didn't diversify investments

Lessons Learned: Mike now studies market trends and only invests what he can afford to lose. His experience shows the importance of research and emotional control in investing.

The Rodriguez Family's Smart Saving

The Rodriguez family wanted to buy their first home but struggled to save money. They created a detailed budget tracking system:

Their Strategy:

- Automated savings transfers on payday
- Cut subscription services
- Started meal planning
- Used cash for discretionary spending

Results: In 18 months, they saved $25,000 for a down payment. Their method demonstrates how small changes add up to significant savings.

Jason's Custom T-Shirts

Jason turned his artistic talent into a business at age 16. He started designing custom t-shirts for school clubs.

Smart Moves:

- Used print-on-demand service
- Created designs during free time
- Marketed through Instagram
- Kept costs low

Impact: Jason earned enough to pay for his first year of college and learned valuable business skills early.

The Smith Small Business Tax Troubles

The Smiths ran a successful bakery but didn't keep good tax records. They faced penalties and stress during tax season.

Problems Faced:

- Mixed personal and business expenses
- Lost important receipts
- Missed quarterly tax payments
- Didn't set aside money for taxes

Resolution: They hired a bookkeeper and implemented a proper accounting system. Their case highlights the importance of good tax management.

Emma's Budget App

Emma struggled with overspending until she switched over to using digital banking tools.

Her System:

- Used app notifications for purchases
- Set up automatic bill payments
- Created digital envelopes for spending
- Tracked expenses in real-time

Outcome: Emma paid off $5,000 in credit card debt in one year using digital tools to control spending.

Discussion Questions:

1. Which case study relates most to your current situation?
2. What specific strategies from these stories could you apply to your life?
3. How might these stories end differently with poor money management?
4. Which case demonstrates the most important money lesson?

Activity:

Create your own money management case study by documenting your financial decisions for one month. Track your choices, challenges, and lessons learned.

Key Takeaways:

- Money evolved over time from barter to digital forms.
- Money can be earned through work, interest, or entrepreneurship.
- Taxes fund essential public services.
- Control your money; don't let it control you.
- Wise money management is crucial.

Chapter 2

Introduction to Financial Independence

Understanding the Concept of Financial Independence

Imagine being able to make choices in life without worrying about money. That's what financial independence means. It means having enough money saved or invested so you can live the life you want.

When you have financial independence, you can decide what to do with your time. Maybe you want to travel, start a business, or help others. Money becomes a tool that helps you reach your goals, not something that holds you back.

Achieving financial independence is a marathon, not a sprint. It doesn't happen overnight. This journey takes planning, saving, and a willingness to learn about money. The good news is, the sooner you start, the easier it can be.

You might wonder how to begin. Start by thinking about your future. What kind of life do you want when you're older? Do you want to own a home, have a car, or maybe start a company? Knowing what you want helps you plan how to get there.

Saving money is a big part of becoming financially independent. Even small amounts saved regularly can grow over time. This is because of something called compound interest. It's when the money you save earns interest, and then that interest earns more interest.

Another important part of the process is understanding how to manage your money. This means knowing exactly how much you earn and how much you spend. Creating a budget can help you keep track. It shows you where your money goes and where you might be able to save more.

Investing is also key to financial independence. Investing is all about putting your money to work, making it grow beyond what simple saving can achieve. It means using your money to make more money. From stocks and bonds to real estate, exploring different investment avenues can significantly accelerate your financial progress.

Being careful with debt is important too. Debt is money you owe to someone else. Some debts, like a student loan or a mortgage, can be useful. But other debts, like credit card debt, can make it harder to reach financial independence. It's best to avoid unnecessary debt when you can.

It's okay to ask for help. Talk to your parents, teachers, or someone you trust about money. They can share their experiences and give advice. There are also many books and online resources that can teach you more.

Why Financial Literacy Is Crucial for Teens

Knowing how to handle money is an important skill. For teens, learning about money now can make all the difference later in life.

Money affects many parts of our lives. It helps us buy things we need and want, and it helps us plan for the future. Understanding money means you can make smart choices.

As a teen, you might have a part-time job or get an allowance. This is a great chance to practice managing money. You can learn now how best to save, spend wisely, and maybe even invest.

Financial literacy means knowing how money works in all of its various forms and functions. It includes things like budgeting, saving, investing, and understanding credit. When you learn these things early, you can avoid mistakes that can cause problems later.

For example, if you know how to budget, you can make sure you don't spend more than you have. This helps you avoid debt. If you understand credit, you can use it wisely and keep a good credit score.

Learning about money can also help you reach your goals effectively. Maybe you want to buy a car, go to college, or travel. Knowing how to save and plan can make these things possible.

Money skills are not always taught in school. That's why it's important to take the time to learn on your own. There are many resources available, like books, websites, and even apps that can teach you.

Being financially literate also means you can help others. You can share what you learn with friends and family, and this can create a positive impact on your community.

Understanding money can also reduce your stress. Money problems are a common cause of worry for many people, adults and teens alike. When you know how to manage your money, you can feel more secure and confident.

Starting to learn about money as a teen gives you more time to grow your savings and investments. Time is a powerful tool in building wealth. The earlier you start, the more your money can grow.

Financial literacy empowers you to make informed decisions. Whether it's choosing a bank account, deciding how to pay for college, or planning for retirement, knowing about money helps you choose what's best for you.

Don't be afraid to ask questions. Talk to adults you trust about money. They can share their experiences and offer information and advice.

Learning about money now will set you up for success in the future. It gives you control over your life and helps you achieve your dreams.

Exploring Khan Academy's Personal Finance Course

Case Studies

1. **Visit Khan Academy**: Go to www.khanacademy.org.
2. **Sign Up or Log In**: Create an account using your email or log in if you already have one.
3. **Access 'Personal Finance'**: In the search bar, type "Personal Finance" and select the course.
4. **Start with Basics**: Begin with the "Welcome to Personal Finance" introduction.
5. **Watch Video Lessons**: Engage with videos on topics like budgeting, saving, and investing.
6. **Take Practice Exercises**: After videos, complete exercises to test your understanding.
7. **Use the Progress Tracker**: Monitor your learning progress through the dashboard.
8. **Set Learning Goals**: Schedule regular times each week to continue the course.
9. **Explore Additional Topics**: Dive into sections on taxes, credit, and insurance.
10. **Discuss with Peers**: Join discussion forums to ask questions and share insights.

Alex's College Early Start Strategy

Alex started planning for financial independence at 16 after learning about compound interest in math class.

Key Actions:

- Saved 50% of part-time job earnings
- Opened a high-yield savings account
- Applied for scholarships aggressively
- Lived at home during college

Results After 4 Years:

- Graduated debt-free
- Had $12,000 in savings
- Built excellent credit score
- Secured high-paying entry-level job

Lesson: Starting early with clear goals can prevent student debt and create a strong financial foundation.

Maria's Side Hustle Journey

Maria, a high school teacher, achieved financial independence through multiple income streams.

Her Strategy:

- Lived on teaching salary
- Tutored online evenings
- Created and sold educational materials
- Invested extra income in index funds

Monthly Breakdown:

- Teaching salary: $4,000
- Online tutoring: $1,200
- Educational materials: $800
- Total investments: $2,000

Impact: Reached financial independence in 8 years, and now works by choice rather than necessity.

David's Minimalist Story

David realized he could reach financial independence faster by reducing expenses rather than just increasing income.

Cost-Cutting Measures:

- Moved to smaller apartment
- Used public transportation
- Cooked meals at home
- Embraced a minimalist lifestyle

Monthly Savings:

- Housing: $600
- Transportation: $400
- Food: $300
- Entertainment: $200

Outcome: Achieved 70% savings rate and reached financial independence in 10 years.

Priya's Tech Fast Track

Priya leveraged her high-paying tech job to reach financial independence quickly.

Financial Plan:

- Lived like a student despite high salary
- Maxed out retirement accounts
- Built emergency fund
- Invested in real estate

Investment Strategy:

- 401(k): $19,500/year
- IRA: $6,000/year
- Real estate: $24,000/year
- Index funds: $30,000/year

Result: Reached financial independence at age 35 through aggressive saving and smart investing.

Thompson Family Journey

The Thompsons achieved financial independence while raising three children.

Family Strategy:

- One parent worked remotely
- Kids involved in financial decisions
- Family entrepreneurship projects
- Shared cost-saving activities

Budget Priorities:

- Education savings first
- Family health insurance

- Emergency fund
- Investment portfolio

Achievement: Reached financial independence when the youngest started college.

Key Takeaways:

- Financial independence offers options.
- Financial literacy leads to smart money decisions.
- Setting financial goals directs your path.

CHAPTER 3

BUILDING A STRONG FINANCIAL FOUNDATION

Basics of Money Management

HANDLING MONEY EFFECTIVELY MIGHT seem tricky at first, but it's a skill anyone can learn. Knowing how to manage your money helps you make better choices and reach your goals faster. Whether you're saving for something special or just want to have extra cash on hand, understanding money is critically important.

Think about the things you want to buy or do. Maybe it's a new phone, a game, or saving for college. Managing money means making a plan for how to use what you have to get what you want. By creating a roadmap for how to use your resources most effectively, you will gain a clear view of your finances and pave the way for success.

One important part of money management is understanding where your money comes from and where it goes. Do you get an allowance? Do you earn money from a part-time job or doing chores? Keeping track of this income helps you see how much you have to work with. It's helpful to write down all the ways you earn money, no matter how small.

Expenses are the things you spend your money on. This can be anything from snacks and clothes to bigger items like electronics. Don't forget to include things like subscription services! Writing down each of your expenses helps you see patterns and decide if you're spending on things that really matter to you. Sometimes, we don't realize how small purchases add up over time.

Saving is another key piece of the financial puzzle. When you set aside some money, you're preparing for future needs or wants. Even small amounts add up over time. For example, saving just $5 a week can become $260 in a year. That's enough for something you've been wanting. Consistent saving empowers you to reach your goals, one step at a time.

Being aware of needs versus wants helps in making smart decisions. Needs are things you must have, like food and school supplies. Wants are nice to have but not necessary, like the latest video game. By focusing on needs first, you ensure that the important things are covered.

Setting financial goals gives you something to work toward. It could be saving for a trip, a special purchase, or just building up your savings. Goals can be short-term or long-term. Write down your goals! This makes them more real and helps you stay focused.

Money management isn't just about spending less. It's about making choices that help you get the most out of what you have. Sometimes spending a little more on a quality item saves money in the long run because it will last longer than something that is more cheaply made.

Unexpected expenses can always come up. Having some savings will help you handle these surprises without stress. This is called an emergency fund. Even a small emergency fund can make a big difference when things don't go as planned.

Talking to family or trusted adults about money can give you new ideas and help you learn from their experiences. They might have tips on how to save, budget, or earn extra money.

There are tools that can help, like apps or simple notebooks, to track your money. Find the methods that work best for you. Some people like using spreadsheets, while others prefer writing things down on paper.

Managing money is a skill that improves with practice. The more you pay attention to it, the better you'll get. Don't get discouraged if it seems hard at first.

Mistakes happen to everyone. The important thing is to learn from them and keep moving forward. If you overspend one week, try to adjust the next week.

Taking control of your finances helps you achieve the things that are important to you. It's empowering to know that you can make your money work for you.

Starting good habits now will help you in the future. The skills you learn today will benefit you throughout your life.

Learning Money Management with Practical Money Skills

1. **Visit Practical Money Skills: Go to www.practicalmoneyskills.com.**
2. **Select 'Students' Section**: Click on "Learn" and choose "Students" from the dropdown.
3. **Choose Your Age Group**: Select the appropriate category (e.g., "Teens").
4. **Explore Learning Modules**: Access topics like budgeting, saving, and financial responsibility.
5. **Download Resources**: Utilize free worksheets and guides available for each topic.
6. **Play Educational Games**: Engage with interactive games like "Financial Football" to make learning fun.
7. **Read Articles**: Stay informed with articles tailored to young adults.
8. **Take Quizzes**: Test your knowledge with quizzes at the end of each module.
9. **Set Personal Goals**: Apply what you've learned by setting your own financial goals.
10. **Share with Friends**: Encourage peers to learn alongside you for mutual sup-

port.

The Importance of Budgeting

Budgeting might sound complicated, but it's simply a plan for how you use your money. Having a budget helps you know exactly where your money is going. This way, you have a clear understanding of your finances.

When you budget, you can make sure you have enough for the things you need and the things you want. It helps prevent running out of money unexpectedly. Planning ahead makes managing money easier.

A budget can help you reach your financial goals faster. By planning your spending, you can set aside money for bigger purchases or savings. This makes it easier to achieve what you've been aiming for.

Budgeting teaches responsibility. It shows you how to make choices and prioritize what's important. This skill is useful not just for money but in other areas of life too.

Without a budget, it's easy to spend money without thinking. You might wonder where all your money went at the end of the month. Keeping track helps prevent this confusion and avoid headaches down the road.

A budget helps you stay out of debt. By knowing your limits, you can prevent borrowing money you can't pay back. This keeps your finances healthy and stress-free.

Budgeting also reduces stress. When you have a plan, you don't have to worry about whether you'll have enough money. This peace of mind allows you to focus on other things.

It's a skill that will benefit you throughout your entire life. Learning to budget now, while you're young and fairly early in the game, prepares you for managing larger amounts of money in the future. Employers and colleges appreciate people who can manage resources well.

Budgeting helps you make better spending decisions, so that you use your money with intention. You'll be more aware of prices and look for ways to save. This can lead to finding great deals and stretching your money further.

Having a budget doesn't mean you can't have fun. It just means you plan for fun expenses so they fit into your overall plan. This way, you can enjoy yourself without worrying about overspending.

Through budgeting you can better understand the value of money. You'll appreciate what things cost and make choices that reflect your values. This awareness can lead to more thoughtful spending.

Sharing your budget with your family can also be a powerful tool. Not only does it help them understand your financial priorities, but it also opens the door for valuable support and collaboration. They might surprise you with some game-changing tips or ideas to help you reach your objectives even faster.

Your budget is a flexible tool that grows with you. You can always adjust it as things change. If you earn more or less, or if your expenses increase, you can update your budget accordingly.

Budgeting isn't about limiting yourself; it's about tracking your money and making work best for you. It's empowering to know that you're in control of your finances.

Starting to budget now sets a strong foundation for your financial future. The more you practice this skill, the better it will serve you in all areas of your life. The habits you build today will serve you well throughout your entire lifetime.

There are different ways to budget. You can use apps, spreadsheets, or just a simple notebook. The important thing is to find a method that you're most comfortable with.

Some people use the envelope system, where they divide cash into different envelopes for different expenses. Others prefer digital methods. Choose what works best for you.

Budgeting is your secret weapon against impulse purchases. It puts you in control and helps you avoid spending recklessly. When you have a plan, you're less likely to spend money on things you don't really need.

It also teaches you to set limits. Knowing exactly how much you have to spend in each category is a good defense against overspending.

Budgeting can even be fun! You can set challenges for yourself, like saving a certain amount each month. Then celebrate your victories and reward yourself when you reach your goals. Having a budget doesn't mean that you can't treat yourself.

Creating a Personal Budget

Making your own budget is a simple process that will help you manage your money more effectively. Here's how you can create a budget that fits your needs.

Start by listing all your sources of income. This could be an allowance, money from a part-time job, or gifts. Write down how much you receive and how often. Knowing your total income is the first step.

Next, list all your expenses. These are the things you spend money on. Include regular expenses like lunch money, transportation, and any subscriptions. Don't forget occasional expenses like birthday gifts or outings with friends.

Now, subtract your total expenses from your total income. This will show you how much money you have left over, and it will let you know whether you're spending more than you have. This step helps you see if your budget is balanced.

If your expenses are more than your income, look for areas where you can cut back. Maybe you can spend less on snacks or wait longer before buying that new game. Adjusting your spending helps balance your budget.

If you have money left over, decide what you want to do with it. You might want to save it, invest it, or set it aside for a future purchase. Planning for extra money prevents it from disappearing without you noticing. This happens quite easily when you are not paying attention, and budgeting is the art of paying careful attention to your resources.

Setting financial goals can help you decide how to use your extra money. Goals give you something to work toward and make budgeting more rewarding. They keep you focused and motivated.

Consider dividing your money into categories. For example, you might allocate money for needs, wants, and savings. A common method using these three categories is the 50/30/20 rule. This is a simple and popular guideline for budgeting money, and you can adjust the percentages to fit your specific situation.

Use tools to help you keep track. There are many budgeting apps designed for teens that make it easy to monitor your spending and savings. Technology can simplify the process.

Review your budget regularly. Things change, and your budget should reflect that. Checking in weekly or monthly helps you stay on track, and regular reviews help you catch any issues early.

Involve your family if you feel comfortable. They can offer advice and support, and they might also understand your financial situation better. Communication can make budgeting easier, and opening up about your budget with family is a great way to foster a feeling of teamwork.

It is important to be honest with yourself about your spending habits. If you notice that you're overspending in certain areas, think about why and how you can adjust. Self-awareness is key to successful budgeting.

Don't forget to include savings in your budget. Even small amounts add up over time, and it just might surprise you to notice this as you start tracking the movement of your money. You might want to open a savings account to keep your money safe. Saving is a crucial part of financial health.

Set reminders to help you stick to your budget. Alerts on your phone or notes in your planner can keep you aware of your spending. Staying mindful helps prevent accidental overspending.

Celebrate your successes. When you reach a savings goal or if you stick to your budget for a month, acknowledge your achievement. Rewards can keep you motivated.

If you find budgeting challenging, start small. Focus on one area of spending and track it for a week. Gradually add more categories as you get comfortable. Taking it step by step makes it less overwhelming.

Remember that it's okay to adjust your budget. If something isn't working, make changes. The goal is to create a budget that helps you, not one that feels restrictive.

Consider needs versus wants when planning your expenses. Prioritize the things you need, and then see what's left for the things you want. This approach ensures that essentials are covered.

Avoid comparing your budget to others. Your budget is a personal roadmap, not a competition. Everyone's financial situation is different. Focus on what works best for you.

Stay motivated by keeping your goals in mind. Visual reminders, like a picture of what you're saving for, can rekindle your enthusiasm when you need it most.

Using Mint to Create and Manage Your Budget

1. **Download Mint App: Install from here.**
2. **Sign Up**: Open the app and create an account with your email and a secure password.
3. **Link Financial Accounts**: Securely connect your bank accounts to track income and expenses.
4. **Set Up Your Profile**: Input basic information to personalize your experience.
5. **Navigate to 'Budgets'**: Tap on the "Budgets" tab to begin setting up.
6. **Add Budget Categories**: Choose from predefined categories or create custom ones.
7. **Set Spending Limits**: Assign monthly limits to each category based on your

income.

8. **Track Transactions**: Review automatically categorized transactions for accuracy.
9. **Monitor Spending**: Check the progress bars to see how much you've spent in each category.
10. **Receive Alerts**: Enable notifications for bill reminders and when nearing budget limits.
11. **Adjust as Needed**: Update your budget regularly to reflect changes in income or expenses.

Exercises:

1. **Income & Expense Tracking**: Record all your income and expenses for two weeks.
2. **Create a Budget**: Use your data to set up a personal monthly budget.
3. **Needs vs. Wants**: List recent purchases and categorize them as needs or wants.
4. **Savings Challenge**: Set a savings goal and adjust your budget to meet it.
5. **Budget Review**: At month's end, evaluate your budget and note improvements.
6. **Financial Goals Vision Board**: Craft a visual board displaying your financial goals.

Case Studies

Thaddeus's Summer Savings Plan

Thaddeus, a 16-year-old high school student, wanted to buy a $600 laptop for his upcoming school year. After tracking his expenses for a month, he realized he was spending most of his part-time job earnings ($200/month) on snacks, movies, and impulse purchases at the mall.

Thaddeus created a detailed budget using a simple notebook. He divided his income into three categories: needs (school supplies and bus fare), wants (entertainment), and savings. He allocated 50% to savings ($100), 30% to needs ($60), and 20% to wants ($40). By cutting back on unnecessary snacks and finding free entertainment options with friends, he stayed within his "wants" budget. After four months, he had saved $400. His parents, impressed by his disciplined saving, offered to contribute the remaining $200 as a reward for his financial responsibility.

Key Lesson: Setting a clear goal and tracking expenses helped Thaddeus understand his spending patterns and make necessary adjustments to achieve his target.

Zephyr's Emergency Fund Experience

Zephyr, a 15-year-old who earned money from mowing lawns, never thought about saving for emergencies until his smartphone broke. Without savings, he had to wait three weeks to save enough for repairs, missing important calls from his weekend job clients.

This experience motivated Zephyr to start an emergency fund. He used the Mint app to track his lawn-mowing income, which varied between $80-200 monthly depending on the season. He committed to saving 25% of each payment for emergencies. When his lawn mower needed repairs two months later, he had $85 saved and could fix it immediately, avoiding lost income from canceled jobs.

Key Lesson: Having an emergency fund helped Zephyr handle unexpected expenses without disrupting his income-earning ability.

Astrid's Budget Evolution

Astrid received a $50 weekly allowance for helping at her family's store. Initially, she spent it all on clothes and accessories, often running out of money before week's end. After learning about budgeting in school, she decided to create a flexible budget that would change with her needs each month.

Using a spreadsheet, Astrid tracked her spending and noticed she needed more money for social activities during school months and more for summer activities during vacation.

She created two different budgets: a school-year budget (40% savings, 40% social activities, 20% personal items) and a summer budget (40% savings, 30% summer activities, 30% personal items).

The dual-budget system helped her maintain consistent savings while realistically planning for different expenses throughout the year. After six months, she had saved $480, which she split between her emergency fund and saving for concert tickets.

Key Lesson: Budgets should be flexible and adjusted based on changing circumstances while maintaining consistent savings habits.

Key Takeaways:

- Track income and expenses to manage money.
- Budgeting plans your spending and saving.
- Personal budgets guide financial choices.

Chapter 4

Tracking Your Money: Using Technology to Manage Finances

Creating a plan for achieving financial goals

Having a plan can make reaching your financial goals easier. It helps you know what steps to take and when to take them. Without a plan, it's harder to see progress and stay motivated.

Make a list of your goals. Write them all down so you can see them. This makes them feel more real. You might have one big goal or several smaller ones.

Figure out how much money you need for each goal. If you want to buy something that costs $200, that's your target amount. Knowing the exact number helps you plan better.

Decide how long you want to take to reach each goal. Maybe you want to save $200 in four months. That means saving $50 each month.

Look at your current income. Do you get an allowance or earn money from a job? Knowing how much money you have coming in helps you figure out how much you can save.

Think about your expenses. Do you spend money on snacks, games, or outings with friends? Knowing where your money goes can help you find ways to save more.

Create a budget. This is a plan for how you'll spend and save your money. Decide how much you'll save each week or month toward your goals.

Try to stick to your budget. It might be hard at first, but it gets easier over time. If you find you're spending too much, look for areas where you can cut back.

Consider setting up a savings account. Putting your money in a safe place can help you avoid spending it on other things. Some banks offer accounts for teens.

Review your plan regularly. Check to see if you're on track to meet your goals. If not, think about what you can change to get back on track and then make those necessary changes.

Be patient with yourself. Sometimes it takes longer than expected to reach a goal. Keep working at it, and don't be too hard on yourself if things don't go perfectly.

Always celebrate your successes! When you reach a goal, take a moment to feel proud of yourself. You've worked hard, and you deserve to enjoy the results.

The importance of ongoing financial education and self-improvement

Learning about money doesn't stop after reading a book or taking a class. There's always more to discover. As you grow older, your financial needs and goals often change.

Staying informed can help you make better decisions. New technologies, including digital payments and cryptocurrencies, are always emerging. Knowing about these can keep you ahead of the game.

Consider reading articles, watching videos, or listening to podcasts about money management. There are many resources available that are made for teens.

Ask questions when you don't understand something. Talking to parents, teachers, or trusted adults can provide helpful insights. They can share their experiences and advice.

Try to learn from your mistakes. If you make a bad purchase or forget to save, think about what happened. Allow yourself to analyze the situation without guilt or self-blame. Understanding where you went wrong can help you avoid similar issues in the future. It's all a learning process. Embrace it!

Set new goals as you achieve old ones. This keeps you motivated and focused on improving. Personal growth is a continuous process.

Stay open to new ideas. The world of finance is always changing. Being willing to learn can help you adapt to new situations and stay ahead of the curve.

Consider joining clubs or groups at school that focus on business or economics. This can be a fun way to learn with friends.

Practice good habits regularly. Saving a portion of your money, budgeting, and thinking before spending are skills that get better with practice.

Learning doesn't have to be boring. Find ways to make it enjoyable. Maybe play financial games or participate in challenges.

Celebrate your wins! Own your progress and recognize how much you've learned and how far you've come. This is a powerful motivator for continued success.

Learning with Next Gen Personal Finance (NGPF)

1. **Visit NGPF**: Go to www.ngpf.org.
2. **Access Student Resources**: Click on "Students" in the top menu.
3. **Explore Online Games**: Engage with interactive games that teach financial concepts.
4. **Watch Video Libraries**: Learn from curated videos on various financial topics.
5. **Take Online Courses**: Enroll in self-paced courses tailored for teens.
6. **Use Financial Calculators**: Experiment with calculators for budgeting, saving,

and investing.

7. **Read Blog Posts**: Stay updated with articles on current financial issues.
8. **Join Webinars**: Participate in live or recorded webinars to deepen your learning.
9. **Connect with Community**: Engage in forums or discussion groups if available.
10. **Set Learning Goals**: Create a plan to cover specific topics each month.

Exercises:

- **Goal Action Plan**: Choose a financial goal and create a detailed action plan with steps, deadlines, and resources needed.
- **Financial Skills Audit**: Assess your current financial skills and identify areas for improvement. Outline how you will develop these skills.
- **Educational Resource List**: Compile a list of five books, websites, or courses to further your financial education.
- **Habit Building Chart**: Create a chart to track daily or weekly financial habits you want to establish, such as saving or budgeting.
- **Peer Learning Group**: Organize a small group discussion with peers to share financial goals and strategies for achieving them.
- **Progress Reflection**: Write a journal entry reflecting on your financial journey so far and how you envision your future.

Case Studies

Pax's Gaming Setup Goal

Pax wanted to build a $1,200 gaming setup but had no savings. Instead of making random purchases, he created a detailed 8-month plan. First, he listed all components: computer

($800), monitor ($250), keyboard ($100), and mouse ($50). From his weekend restaurant job, he earned $400 monthly.

He analyzed his spending and found he was using $200 on food delivery and in-app purchases. By cutting these to $50 monthly, he could save $350 each month. To stay motivated, he created a visual tracker in his room, coloring in sections as he saved. His plan worked - he bought each component in order of importance, starting with the computer. The process taught him patience and the value of systematic saving.

Key Lesson: Breaking down large goals into smaller components and tracking progress visually can make big financial goals achievable.

Vesper's College Fund Journey

Vesper, age 14, learned her dream college would cost $5,000 for the first semester's books and supplies. Rather than feeling overwhelmed, she developed a three-year plan. She combined multiple income sources: babysitting ($100/month), selling custom artwork online ($150/month), and birthday money ($500/year).

She created specific monthly targets: 70% of income to college fund, 20% to current needs, and 10% to her "fun fund." She kept three separate jars at home, physically dividing her money when received. By putting all her birthday and holiday money into savings, plus her regular income splitting, she reached her goal two months early.

Key Lesson: Multiple income streams and consistent saving percentages can help reach long-term financial goals.

Caspian's Market Venture

Caspian wanted to start a weekend market stall selling homemade jewelry, requiring $600 startup costs. He created a detailed 4-month plan, breaking down expenses: supplies ($300), display items ($200), and market fees ($100).

His monthly allowance was $100, but he negotiated with his parents to earn extra by taking on more household responsibilities. They agreed to pay him $50 monthly for maintaining their garden. He also sold unused items from his room, making $200. Each week, he reviewed his progress using a simple spreadsheet.

After three months, he had $450 saved. His grandmother, impressed by his initiative and planning, offered the final $150 as an early birthday gift. Caspian's market stall now generates enough profit to sustain itself, and he's planning to expand his inventory.

Key Lesson: Creating detailed expense breakdowns and finding creative ways to increase income can turn business goals into reality.

Key Takeaways:

- Technology simplifies money management.
- Digital tools track spending and saving.
- Real-time tracking boosts financial awareness.

CHAPTER 5

SMART SAVING: STRATEGIES FOR BUILDING WEALTH

The power of saving early

YOU MIGHT THINK THAT putting away a bit of money isn't important, but it can truly change your life. When you start saving at a young age, your money has more time to grow. Over the years, even small amounts can add up to something big.

Simply saving just a few dollars each week can make a big difference. After some time, those dollars turn into hundreds, then thousands. This happens because of something called interest. Interest is extra money that the bank gives you for keeping your money with them. The longer your money stays in the bank, the more interest you earn.

Suppose you save $10 each week. In a year, you would have $520. If you keep doing this, after ten years, you would have $5,200, not counting the extra interest you earn. This shows how small amounts can grow over time.

There's something else that helps your money grow faster: compound interest. This means you earn interest not only on the money you save but also on the interest you've already earned. It's like a snowball that gets bigger as it rolls down a hill.

For example, if you have $1,000 in the bank, and it earns 2% interest each year, after the first year, you will have $1,020. The next year, you earn interest on $1,020, not just $1,000. Over time, this makes your money grow faster.

When you begin early, your money has more time to benefit from compound interest. Time is your best friend when it comes to saving. The sooner you start, the more your money can grow.

Some people wait until they are older to start saving, but starting now is a much better strategy. Even if you can't set aside very much right now, , every little bit helps. It's about building the habit of saving money.

Think about something you really want in the future. Maybe it's a car, college, or even a trip. Saving now can help you get those things later. It's a great feeling to know that you are actively building the future you want.

Saving money also fosters responsibility and equips you with essential money management skills. This is a lifelong asset that will serve you well into your retirement years.

You don't have to do it alone. It's a good idea to talk to your parents or a trusted adult about how to start saving. They can help you open a savings account and show you how to keep track of your money.

There are also apps and tools that can help you save. Some apps round up your purchases to the nearest dollar and save the extra change for you. This makes saving automatic and easy.

Today's decisions shape tomorrow's reality. The future isn't something that just happens; it is built brick by brick, with each decision you make over time. Saving money now lays a strong foundation for what is to come.

Different types of bank/savings accounts

Banks offer different types of accounts to help you manage and grow your money. Understanding these accounts can help you choose the best one for your needs.

A checking account is a place where you can keep your money for everyday use. It allows you to deposit money, write checks, and use a debit card. This account makes it easy to pay for day-to-day expenses.

A savings account is exactly as it sounds. It is designed to help you save money over time. It usually pays interest, which means you earn a little bit extra just for keeping your money in the bank. It is a great way to let your money grow while it sits in the account. Savings accounts often have limits on how often you can take money out, so they are good for money you want to save for later.

Some banks offer youth savings accounts just for kids and teens. These accounts help you learn how to save and manage money. They might have lower fees and special features to make saving easier.

Certificates of deposit, or CDs, are another option. With a CD, you agree to leave your money in the bank for a set amount of time, like six months or a year. In return, the bank gives you a higher interest rate. This means your money can grow even faster, but you can't take it out until the time is up. It's a good plan for money that you don't intend to touch for a while.

A money market account usually pays more interest than a regular savings account. It might require a higher minimum balance, which means you need to keep more money in the account. This type of account can be a good option if you have more money to save.

Some banks also offer online savings accounts. These accounts are managed over the internet and often pay higher interest rates because the bank saves money on costs like branches and staff.

Choosing the right account depends on your goals. If you need quick access to your money, a checking account might be best. If you want to save money over time, a savings account could be a good choice.

It's important to compare different banks and accounts. Look at things like interest rates, fees, and minimum balances. Some banks charge fees if your account falls below a certain amount.

Opening a bank account is a big step towards managing your money. It helps you keep your money safe and gives you tools to save and spend wisely. Don't hesitate to talk it over with a trusted adult to help you understand the options available and choose the right account for your needs.

Some banks offer apps and online tools to help you track your money. These tools can show you how much you have saved and help you work toward goals.

The bank is there to help you with your money. Don't be afraid to ask questions. The more you know, the better choices you can make.

Opening a Teen Savings Account with Capital One

1. **Visit Capital One**: Go to www.capitalone.com/bank/savings-accounts/kids-savings-account.
2. **Click 'Open Account'**: Begin the application process by selecting "Open Account."
3. **Choose Account Type**: Select "Kids Savings Account" for teens under 18.
4. **Fill Out Application**: Enter personal information with a parent or guardian present.
5. **Provide Identification**: Have your Social Security number and ID documents ready.
6. **Set Up Account Access**: Create login credentials for online banking.
7. **Fund the Account**: Make an initial deposit via bank transfer or check.

8. **Review Terms**: Read the account disclosures and agree to the terms.
9. **Submit Application**: Complete the process and await confirmation.
10. **Download Mobile App**: Install the Capital One app to manage your savings on the go.
11. **Set Savings Goals**: Use account features to set and track financial goals.

Automated saving techniques and tools - tips and tricks

Saving money can be made easier by using tools that automate the process. These tools help you save without even having to think about it.

One way to automate your savings is by setting up automatic transfers. This means your bank moves money from your checking account to your savings account on a regular schedule. For example, you can set it to transfer $10 every week.

Some banks offer programs that round up your purchases. When you buy something, the bank rounds up the amount to the nearest dollar and puts the extra change into your savings account. This way, you save small amounts without noticing.

There are also apps that help you save money automatically. Apps like Acorns and Digit connect to your bank account and move small amounts into savings or investments. These apps make saving easy and fun.

Using automatic saving tools helps you build good habits and set aside money almost effortlessly. You don't have to remember to save; the tools do it for you. Over time, these small amounts can add up to big savings.

Setting specific savings goals can also help you level up your money management game. Decide what you are saving for and how much you need. Some apps let you create goals and track your progress. Seeing how close you are to your goal can motivate you to keep saving.

Another tip is to save part of any money you receive. If you get birthday money or earn cash from a job, put some of it into savings before you spend it. This helps your savings grow faster. You can decide on a standard percentage or amount to help this habit become automatic. For example, committing to saving 10% of any money you get can really add up over time.

Keeping your savings in a separate account can help you avoid spending it. When your spending money and savings are in different places, it's easier to see how much you have saved and allow it to keep growing.

Don't underestimate the power of talking to your parents! They can help you design a plan for earning and saving, from setting up an allowance to offering you paid chores or jobs around the house. They can also point you toward the most effective tools and apps to use.

Making saving automatic takes the effort out of it. It allows you to focus on other things while your money grows in the background. However, it's still important to check in on your accounts regularly. Keeping track of what your money is doing helps you stay on top of your savings.

If you find saving hard, just start small and keep it simple. Even saving a few dollars a week makes a difference over time. A simple plan with a little support can go a long way. Setting up reminders or using apps with helpful notifications can help you stay on track and stay encouraged.

It's important to find tools and methods that work for you. Everyone is different, so try different things to see what helps you save the best.

Automate Savings with Acorns

1. **Download Acorns**: Install from here.

2. **Sign Up**: Open the app and create an account with your email and a password.

3. **Verify Identity**: Provide necessary personal information for security purposes.
4. **Link a Funding Source**: Connect your checking account or debit card.
5. **Enable Round-Ups**: Turn on the feature to round up purchases and invest the spare change.
6. **Choose an Investment Portfolio**: Select a portfolio based on your risk tolerance.
7. **Set Recurring Investments**: Optionally, schedule automatic deposits to boost savings.
8. **Review Account**: Monitor your investment performance within the app.
9. **Access Educational Content**: Learn more about investing through articles and videos.
10. **Secure Your Account**: Enable security features like PIN or biometric login.

Exercises:

1. **Compound Interest Exercise**: Calculate how $500 grows over 5 years at 2% annual interest compounded yearly.
2. **Account Research**: Compare checking, savings, and youth accounts at two banks.
3. **Automate Savings**: If possible, set up an automatic transfer to your savings account.
4. **Savings Tracker**: Design a chart to monitor your savings toward a goal.
5. **Interest Rate Impact**: Research current savings interest rates and discuss their effect on your savings.
6. **Savings Habit List**: Identify daily habits that can help increase your savings.

Case Studies

Zara's Compound Interest Discovery

Zara received $200 for her 13th birthday. Rather than spending it immediately, she researched different savings options. After comparing several banks, she found a youth savings account offering 3% interest compounded monthly. She deposited her birthday money and committed to adding $20 monthly from her allowance. By tracking her account through the bank's app, she watched in amazement as her money grew not just from her deposits, but also from the compound interest. After two years, her initial $200 had grown to nearly $800. This motivated her to increase her monthly savings to $30, understanding that time and compound interest were working together to help her money grow.

Orion's Account Strategy

Orion wanted to manage his money better but kept spending his savings. He decided to open two accounts: a checking account for daily expenses and a separate high-yield savings account at an online bank. The online savings account had no ATM access, making it harder to spend impulsively. He set up his part-time job paychecks to automatically deposit 75% into his savings account and 25% into checking. He chose the online bank because it offered 2.5% interest compared to his local bank's 0.5%. After eight months, Orion had accumulated $2,400 in his savings account, including $42 in interest earnings.

Phoenix's Automated Success

Phoenix struggled to save consistently until discovering automated saving tools. She started using an app that rounded up her purchases to the nearest dollar and saved the difference. When she bought lunch for $7.25, the app rounded up to $8 and saved $0.75. She also set up weekly automated transfers of $15 from her allowance to savings. The app showed her daily progress with colorful graphs, making saving feel like a game. In six months, her round-ups alone saved $284, while her automated transfers added another $390. This passive approach to saving helped Phoenix reach her goal of buying a new laptop without feeling deprived of spending money.

Key Takeaways:

- Early saving leverages compound interest.
- Different accounts meet different needs.
- Automating saves money effortlessly.

CHAPTER 6

PLANNING FOR MAJOR EXPENSES

Saving for college or vocational training

THINKING ABOUT WHAT COMES after high school can be exciting and a bit overwhelming. Whether you're considering college or vocational training, it's important to start planning now. Setting aside money for your future education can make a big difference when the time comes.

One way to begin is by opening a savings account specifically for your education. Even if you can only deposit a small amount each month, it will add up over time. Remember that small steps today can lead to big results later on.

Another idea is to look for part-time jobs or side gigs. Babysitting, mowing lawns, or even selling handmade crafts can help you earn extra cash. Putting some of that money into your education fund shows that you're serious about achieving your goals.

It's also helpful to learn about scholarships and grants. Many organizations offer financial assistance to students. Doing some research now can uncover opportunities you might not have known about.

Talking to your family can provide more support. They might be able to provide fresh ideas or additional resources to help on your saving journey. Sometimes, relatives are willing to contribute to your education fund instead of giving traditional gifts.

Setting clear goals is a great way to stay motivated. Decide how much you want to save by a certain date. Writing down your goals and tracking your progress makes it easier to stay on track.

Avoid unnecessary spending whenever possible. Before making a purchase, ask yourself if it's something you truly need. Saving money on small expenses leaves more for your education fund.

Consider starting a hobby that doesn't cost much. Activities like reading, drawing, or playing sports can be enjoyable without breaking the bank. Finding fun in simple things is another way to help you save more.

Learning about budgeting can make saving easier and help you plan for life after high school. Create a simple budget that shows your income and expenses. Seeing where your money goes helps you make better choices now, so that you set yourself up for success in the future.

Don't ever be afraid to ask for advice. Teachers, counselors, or mentors might have tips on planning for your future education. Many of them have been through the process of saving and paying for education, and their experience could really benefit you as you plan. They can share their insights and guide you in the right direction.

Celebrating your progress is important. Saving money isn't always easy, but every dollar counts. Reward yourself when you reach a milestone, even if it's something small.

Thinking ahead shows maturity and responsibility. By taking steps now to save for college or vocational training, you're investing in your future. The effort you put in today can open doors to opportunities tomorrow.

Exploring different savings options can also benefit you. Check with your local banks today, as some offer special accounts with higher interest rates for students. This means your money has the opportunity to grow even faster. Understanding how interest works can also boost your savings. Interest is a reward from the bank for keeping your money there. The more you save, the more interest you earn.

It's important to stay focused on your goal. Remember your goal as you make decisions in your daily life. Sometimes, friends might invite you to activities that cost money. It's okay to say no or suggest a less expensive alternative.

Volunteering can be another great way to work towards your future. Some scholarships consider community service experience when choosing recipients. Plus, helping others feels good and builds character.

Keep an eye out for educational programs that offer free or low-cost classes! Learning new skills now not only prepares you for college or vocational training, but it also helps you develop a lifelong learning mindset. Community centers, libraries, and online learning platforms often host workshops, courses, and training sessions on a wide range of subjects.

Beyond educational opportunities, there are other practical steps you can take to improve your financial situation. For example, consider selling items you no longer need. Old clothes, games, or gadgets can bring in extra cash. Clearing out clutter helps you stay organized too.

Stay positive and believe in yourself. Saving for education might seem challenging, but your efforts will pay off. Every bit you save brings you closer to your dream.

Create a vision board or a journal to remind yourself of your goals. Visual reminders are a powerful tool to keep you inspired and on track.

Remember that you're not alone in this journey. Many teens are working towards similar goals. Sharing ideas and supporting each other can make the process more enjoyable.

Keep yourself informed about changes in education costs. Tuition fees and expenses can vary and often increase over time, so knowing the latest information will help you plan better.

Be proud of what you're doing! Saving for your future shows responsibility and determination. Your hard work now will lead to exciting opportunities ahead.

Starting a 529 College Savings Plan

1. **Research 529 Plans**: Visit www.savingforcollege.com to compare options.
2. **Select a Plan**: Choose your state's 529 plan or one that suits your needs.
3. **Go to Plan's Website**: Access the plan's official site through provided links.
4. **Begin Enrollment**: Click on "Open an Account" or similar to start.
5. **Complete Application**: Enter required information about the account owner and beneficiary.
6. **Choose Investment Options**: Select investment portfolios based on risk preference.
7. **Fund the Account**: Make an initial contribution using bank transfer or check.
8. **Set Up Automatic Contributions**: Schedule regular deposits to grow savings over time.
9. **Review and Confirm**: Check all details and submit the application.
10. **Monitor Account**: Log in periodically to track progress and make adjustments.
11. **Learn About Tax Benefits**: Understand any state tax deductions or credits available.

Budgeting for a car or other major purchases

Getting your first car or making a big purchase can be an exciting milestone. Planning ahead will help you achieve this goal without unnecessary stress. Creating a budget is always a smart way to manage your money and save up for what you want.

Practice this process as you plan for each new big expense. Start by figuring out how much money you have coming in, including allowances, part-time job earnings, or gifts. Knowing your income helps you understand how much you can save each month.

Then make a list of your expenses, so you can see where your money goes and find areas where you can cut back.

Setting a savings goal is the next step. Decide how much you need for your car or other large purchase. Break it down into smaller, manageable amounts to save each week or month.

Finding creative ways to earn extra money can help boost your savings. Consider taking on additional chores, offering tutoring services, or starting a small business like dog walking.

Keeping track of your spending is important. Use a notebook or a simple app to record every time you spend money. This helps you stay aware of your habits and make better choices.

Additionally, for larger expenses like saving for college or a vehicle. also wise to research the costs involved. For a car, this includes not just the purchase price, but also insurance, fuel, and maintenance. Understanding the full cost helps you plan more accurately.

Talk to people who have made similar purchases. Your friends or family members might have tips on finding good deals or avoiding common pitfalls. They might be able to refer you to reputable sellers or support you with your savings plan.

Being patient is key. Saving for a big purchase takes time, but sticking to your plan will get you there. Avoid impulse buys that can derail your budget. You have the power to achieve what you want.

Consider opening a separate savings account for your goal. Keeping this money separate from your daily spending or other savings can reduce temptation to use it for other things.

Look for opportunities to save money on everyday expenses. Evaluate your habits and see where you might be able to save resources. Packing your lunch instead of buying it or choosing free activities with friends can add up over time.

Don't be discouraged by setbacks. If unexpected expenses come up, adjust your budget and keep moving forward. Flexibility is part of the process. Planning for major purchases teaches valuable life skills. Budgeting, saving, and making informed decisions will benefit you now and in the future.

Learning about basic car maintenance can also save you money in the long run. Simple tasks such as checking the oil or tire pressure can prevent bigger problems later. Having an awareness of regular car care helps you get every mile out of the vehicle you saved hard to get.

Exploring used options can be a smart choice. A pre-owned car or item can be more affordable while still meeting your needs. Just make sure to check the condition carefully.

Consider the timing of your purchase. Sometimes, waiting for sales or discounts can save you money. Being patient can really pay off!

Think about the long-term value of what you're buying. Will it still be useful in a few years? Investing in quality can be better than going for the cheapest option.

Learn about negotiation skills. When buying a car or big item, sometimes the price isn't set in stone. Knowing how to negotiate can help you get a better deal.

Stay informed about any additional fees or taxes. These costs can add up, so include them in your budget.It is also important to look into warranties or return policies. Understanding these details can protect you if something goes wrong with your purchase.

Avoid borrowing money if at all possible. Taking on debt can often lead to stress and extra costs due to interest. Saving steadily is the smart plan to help you purchase items outright and avoid the pitfalls of debt.

If you do need to borrow, make sure you understand the terms completely. Only agree to what you can realistically pay back in a reasonable amount of time

Consider teaming up with a friend or sibling if appropriate. Sharing the cost might make the purchase more achievable.And keep your eyes open for community resources. Sometimes, there are programs that help teens with big purchases.

Stay organized by keeping all your receipts and paperwork. This will help if any issues arise later.Reflect on why you want this purchase. Make sure it's something that will truly add value to your life. Write down your thoughts as you carefully consider your decision.

Understanding loans and financing options

Sometimes, big purchases require more money than you have saved. Understanding loans and financing options can help you make informed decisions. Knowing how borrowing works is important to avoid problems later on.

Loans are amounts of money you borrow and agree to pay back over time. This usually includes interest, which is an extra amount charged by the lender. It's important to know how much you'll owe in total.

There are different types of loans. For example, student loans help pay for education, while car loans are for buying vehicles. Each type has its own terms and conditions.

Before taking a loan, it's wise to consider whether you really need it. Borrowing money means you have a responsibility to pay it back, often with interest. Understanding interest rates is crucial. A higher interest rate means you'll pay more overall for your purchase. Comparing rates from different lenders can save you money.

It's also important to look at the loan term. This is how long you have to repay the loan. Longer terms might mean smaller monthly payments but more interest paid overall.

Reading the fine print is necessary. Some loans have hidden fees or penalties for paying off early. Knowing all the details helps you avoid surprises.

Credit cards are another form of borrowing. While they can be convenient, they often come with high interest rates if you don't pay the full balance each month.

Building good credit is helpful for future borrowing. Paying bills on time and keeping debts low can improve your credit score.

If you're considering a loan, talking to a trusted adult or financial advisor is a good idea. They can help you understand the terms and decide if it's the right choice.

Sometimes, saving a bit longer can help you avoid borrowing altogether. Patience can save you money and stress.

If you do decide to borrow, make a plan for how you'll repay the loan. Budgeting for the payments and making them on time ensures you stay on track.

Be cautious of predatory lenders. These are companies that offer loans with unfair terms that can trap you in debt. Always research and choose reputable lenders.

Understanding collateral is also important. Some loans require you to offer something valuable as security. This means that if you can't repay, the lender can take this item.

Consider alternatives to loans when possible. Grants, scholarships, or saving up might be better options depending on your situation.

Educate yourself about financial terms. Knowing words such as *principal*, *interest*, and *annual percentage rate* (APR) can help you make better choices.

Borrowing affects your future finances. Making responsible decisions now can prevent problems down the road. Delaying purchases until you have saved the full amount can help you avoid borrowing.

Exploring government programs or community assistance can provide help without the need for loans. Sometimes, there are resources available for teens that can reduce costs.

Think about the impact of debt on your life. Owing money can limit your freedom and choices in the future. Keeping debt low gives you more options.

Learn about the difference between good debt and bad debt. Good debt is borrowing for things that can increase your value, such as education. Bad debt is borrowing for things that lose value quickly.

Be aware of scams and offers that seem too good to be true. Always verify information and avoid sharing personal details with untrusted sources.

Understand that defaulting on a loan, which means failing to repay, can have serious consequences. It can damage your credit and make it harder to borrow in the future.

Consider setting up automatic payments to avoid missing due dates. Staying organized helps you manage your responsibilities.

If you get into trouble with debt, seek help early. There are counselors and services that can assist you in finding solutions. Educate yourself continuously. Financial literacy is a valuable skill that will serve you throughout your life.

Practice negotiating terms if possible. Sometimes, lenders are willing to adjust interest rates or payment schedules.

Keep records of all your loan documents and communications and store them in a secure place. This information is important if questions or issues arise.

It's okay to say no. If a loan doesn't feel right or the terms are unfavorable, you don't have to accept it. Shop around for the best deal.

Federal Student Aid

1. **Visit Federal Student Aid: Go to studentaid.gov.**
2. **Click on 'Apply for Aid'**: Navigate to the "FAFSA® Form" section.
3. **Learn About FAFSA®**: Read about the Free Application for Federal Student Aid.

4. **Use the FAFSA® Demo Site**: Access the demo to familiarize yourself with the application process.
5. **Explore Aid Options**: Under "Types of Aid," read about grants, loans, and work-study programs.
6. **Calculate Aid Eligibility**: Use the "Federal Student Aid Estimator" to get an idea of potential aid.
7. **Read About Loan Repayment**: Understand how student loan repayment works after graduation.
8. **Check Deadlines**: Note important dates for FAFSA® submission in your state.
9. **Create an FSA ID**: When ready, set up an FSA ID for future applications.
10. **Discuss with a Counselor**: Talk to a school counselor for personalized guidance.

Exercises:

1. **Education Cost Research**: Find out the total cost of a college or vocational program you're interested in.
2. **Big Purchase Plan**: Develop a savings plan for a major item you want in the next two years.
3. **Loan Comparison**: Compare a student loan and a car loan—interest rates and repayment terms.
4. **Scholarship Search**: Identify three scholarships you can apply for and their criteria.
5. **Budget Adjustment**: Modify your budget to include savings for a major expense.
6. **Loan Repayment Calculation**: Calculate total repayment on a $10,000 loan at 5% interest over 5 years.

Case Studies

Sage's First Car Journey

Sage wanted to buy a $4,500 used truck for his landscaping business idea. He mapped out a 12-month plan, calculating he needed to save $375 monthly. Through his current lawn mowing service, he had been earning $200 monthly. To bridge the gap, he started helping his neighbor restore vintage furniture, earning an extra $200 monthly. He opened a dedicated savings account and automatically transferred 90% of his earnings. By avoiding unnecessary purchases and selling his old gaming equipment for $400, he reached his goal one month early. He also saved an additional $500 for insurance and maintenance costs.

Blade's Photography Equipment Plan

Blade needed $2,800 for professional camera equipment to start a weekend photography business. Instead of borrowing money, he created a six-month savings strategy. He worked weekends at a local diner earning $600 monthly and allocated 70% to his equipment fund. He also sold his unused electronics and clothes online, making $400. By cooking meals at home instead of buying lunch at school, he was able to save an extra $60 monthly. After reaching $2,000, his grandfather matched his final $800 as an investment in his business idea, allowing him to purchase his equipment debt-free.

Echo's Home Recording Studio

Echo dreamed of building a $3,200 home recording studio. She tracked her spending and discovered she was spending $150 monthly on takeout and streaming services. After cutting these expenses down to $50, she put the savings toward her studio fund. She also started offering virtual music theory lessons, earning $200 monthly. Instead of keeping cash at home, she opened a high-yield savings account paying 2% interest. When a local music store announced a 15% discount on equipment, she had saved enough to purchase everything she needed and still had $300 left for acoustic foam panels. Her careful planning allowed her to build her studio without any loans.

Key Takeaways:

- Plan ahead for big expenses like education.

- Budgeting helps save for large goals.
- Understand loans to make informed choices.

CHAPTER 7

MANAGING DEBT WISELY

Types of Debt and Their Implications

MONEY HELPS YOU BUY the things you need and want. Sometimes, you might not have enough money right away. When this happens, people often think about borrowing. Borrowing means getting money now and agreeing to pay it back later. This borrowed money is called debt.

There are different kinds of debt. One kind is called good debt. Good debt is borrowing money for something that can help you in the future. For example, taking out a loan to pay for college can be good debt because education can lead to better job opportunities.

Another kind is bad debt. Bad debt is when you borrow money for things that don't help you in the long run. Using a credit card to buy expensive shoes you don't need can be bad debt. This kind of debt doesn't bring lasting value.

Some debts are secured. Secured debt means you promise to give up something valuable if you can't pay back the loan. When your parents get a loan to buy a house, the house is the security. If they can't pay back the loan, the bank can take the house.

Other debts are unsecured. Unsecured debt means there's no promise of valuable items. Credit cards are usually unsecured debt. If you don't pay back what you owe, the bank can't take your belongings, but they can still cause problems for you.

When you borrow money, you have to pay back the amount you borrowed plus extra money called interest. Interest is a fee for borrowing the money. The longer you take to pay it back, the more interest you will owe.

High-interest debt means you have to pay back a lot more than you borrowed. Credit cards often have high interest rates. If you only pay a little each month, it can take a very long time to pay off the debt.

Low-interest debt means you pay back less extra money. Student loans sometimes have low interest rates, making them easier to manage over time.

Having too much debt can cause stress. It might be hard to pay for other things you need if you owe a lot of money. Some people have to work extra jobs to pay off their debts.

Borrowing money affects your credit score. A credit score is a number that shows how good you are at paying back money. If you have a good credit score, banks are more likely to lend you money in the future.

Not paying back debt on time can make your credit score go down. A low credit score can make it harder to get loans when you need them.

Understanding the different types of debt helps you make smart choices. Before borrowing money, think about why you need it and how you will pay it back. Consider whether you might be able to save a while longer instead of taking on the burden of debt.

It's important to borrow only what you can afford to repay. Always read the terms of any loan or credit card carefully. If something is confusing, ask questions.

Debt can be a helpful tool when used wisely. It can help you buy a home or pay for education. But it can also cause problems if not managed carefully.

Being cautious with borrowing now can save you from trouble later. Making smart decisions about debt will help you build a strong financial future.

Strategies for Avoiding Debt Traps

Debt traps are situations where it's hard to pay back what you owe. They can happen when borrowing becomes too easy or when expenses pile up. Here are ways to avoid getting caught in debt traps.

Making a budget is a good start. A budget is a plan for how to spend your money. Write down how much money you have and what you need to spend it on. This helps you see where your money goes and to ensure that it's going where you need it.

Saving money is extremely important. Even small amounts add up over time. Having savings can help you pay for unexpected expenses without needing to borrow.

Always think carefully before spending. It can be tempting to buy new things, but if you can't afford them, it's better to wait.

Be cautious with credit cards. It's easy to swipe a card and buy things, but remember that you have to pay back the money later, often with interest.

If borrowing is absolutely necessary, look for loans with low interest rates. This means you'll pay back less extra money over time.

Paying bills on time is crucial. Late fees can add up and make it harder to pay back what you owe. Setting reminders can help you stay on track.

Avoid taking on too many loans at once. The more debt you have, the harder it is to keep track of payments and stay organized.

Learning to say no to things you don't need will save you money. It's okay to skip buying something if doing so will cause money problems.

Understanding how money works helps you make better choices. Educating yourself now can prevent debt problems later. Seeking advice and information from people you trust is another great strategy for avoiding debt traps. Learning from other people's mistakes and successes can help you make good decisions.

Keeping track of your spending is a key piece of the puzzle. There are apps and tools that can help you see exactly where your money goes each month.Setting financial goals will give you something to work toward. Whether it's saving for a bike or college, goals help you stay focused on gaining the outcomes you desire.

Avoid borrowing money to pay off other debts. This creates a dangerous debt cycle that's tough to escape and can snowball surprisingly quickly.

Being aware of scams and offers that seem too good to be true is important. Sometimes, people try to trick others into bad financial deals for their own benefit.

Asking questions when you're unsure is always a good idea. There are teachers, parents, and other adults who can help you understand.

Staying out of debt traps takes effort, but it's completely worth it. Making smart choices now can lead to a brighter financial future.

Managing Debt with Undebt.it

1. **Visit Undebt.it: Go to www.undebt.it.**
2. **Sign Up**: Create a free account using your email.
3. **Input Debts**: Enter details of any existing debts (amount, interest rate, minimum payment).
4. **Choose a Payoff Method**: Select strategies like Debt Snowball or Debt Avalanche.
5. **Set Payment Goals**: Define how much you can pay monthly towards debts.
6. **Review Payoff Plan**: See a projected timeline for becoming debt-free.
7. **Track Progress**: Update your account as you make payments.

8. **Adjust Plans if Needed**: Modify strategies based on changes in your finances.

9. **Access Tools and Reports**: Utilize graphs and summaries to stay motivated.

10. **Educate Yourself**: Read blog posts and resources on avoiding debt pitfalls.

How to Responsibly Use Credit Cards

Credit cards can be helpful tools if used carefully. They allow you to buy things now and pay for them later. But it's important to use them responsibly to avoid problems. Only use a credit card for things you can afford. If you wouldn't buy it with cash, think twice before charging it.

Try to pay off the full balance each month instead of just the minimum payment. This means paying back fully all the money you spent on the card every month. Doing this helps you avoid paying extra money in interest. If you can't pay off the full balance each month, pay as much as you can. Paying more than the minimum amount helps reduce the interest you'll pay over time.

Keep track of what you spend. It's easy to lose track when using a card. Writing down purchases or using an app can help you stay organized. Set a spending limit for yourself. Decide how much you can spend each month and stick to that amount. Avoid using a credit card to get cash from an ATM. This usually comes with high fees and higher interest rates.

Read your credit card statements carefully. Check for any charges you don't recognize. If something doesn't look right, contact the credit card company.

Protect your credit card information. Don't ever share your card number with people you don't trust. Be careful when using your card online.

Remember that using a credit card affects your credit score. Paying on time and not using too much of your credit limit can help your score stay high. Avoid using multiple credit cards. Managing several cards can be confusing and can lead to more debt. This could negatively affect your credit score in the long run.

Using a credit card can help you build a good credit history if used responsibly. This can make it easier to get loans in the future.

Understanding the terms and conditions of your credit card is important. Know what the interest rates are and any fees that might be charged. Being responsible with a credit card now sets good habits for the future. It teaches you how to manage money and make wise choices.

Monitoring Credit with Credit Karma

1. **Visit Credit Karma**: Go to www.creditkarma.com or download the app.
2. **Sign Up**: Create a free account with your email and password.
3. **Verify Identity**: Provide personal information for security purposes.
4. **Review Credit Scores**: Access your TransUnion and Equifax credit scores.
5. **Understand Credit Factors**: Learn what affects your credit score through detailed breakdowns.
6. **Monitor Accounts**: See all your linked credit accounts in one place.
7. **Set Up Alerts**: Enable notifications for changes to your credit report.
8. **Explore Educational Resources**: Read articles on responsible credit use.
9. **Use Credit Simulator**: Experiment with scenarios to see how actions affect your score.
10. **Plan for Improvement**: Set goals to build or maintain good credit.

Exercises:

1. **Debt Classification**: Identify and list five types of debt (e.g., student loans, credit card debt, mortgage, car loan, payday loans). Categorize each as 'good debt' or 'bad debt' and explain your reasoning.

2. **Interest Calculation**: Suppose you have a credit card balance of $500 with an annual interest rate of 20%. Calculate how much interest you will owe after one year if no payments are made.

3. **Debt Trap Avoidance Plan**: Write down five strategies you can use to avoid falling into debt traps. Explain how each strategy can help maintain financial health.

4. **Credit Card Simulation**: Create a mock monthly budget where you use a credit card for purchases. Include how you plan to pay off the balance each month to avoid interest charges.

5. **Credit Score Impact Study**: Research how missing a credit card payment can affect your credit score. Summarize your findings in a short paragraph.

6. **Role-Playing Exercise**: Imagine a friend is considering taking on high-interest debt for a non-essential purchase. Write a dialogue where you advise them on managing debt wisely.

Case Studies

Kim's Credit Card Lesson

Kim received his first credit card with a $1,000 limit at age 18. Excited by the newfound purchasing power, he quickly spent $800 on gaming equipment and clothes. When the bill arrived, he could only afford the $25 minimum payment. After three months of minimum payments, he realized he had paid $60 in interest charges but only reduced his balance by $40. This wake-up call prompted him to pick up extra shifts at work and cut back on entertainment expenses. He committed to paying $200 monthly until the debt was cleared, and created a rule to only use his credit card for emergencies or planned purchases he could pay off immediately.

Rayne's Debt Comparison

Rayne wanted to purchase a $2,000 laptop for graphic design work. She compared three options: a high-interest store credit card (25% APR), a personal loan from her local bank (12% APR), and a six-month installment plan through her part-time employer (0% interest). After calculating the total cost including interest for each option, she discovered the store card would cost an extra $500 in interest, the bank loan $240, while the employer plan had no extra charges. She chose the employer plan and set up automatic payments from her paycheck. This experience taught her the importance of comparing interest rates and understanding the true cost of borrowing.

Atlas's Debt Prevention Strategy

Atlas watched his older sibling struggle with credit card debt and decided to create a preventive plan. He opened a checking account with a debit card and a separate savings account for emergencies. Whenever he wanted to make a purchase over $100, he implemented a 48-hour waiting period to avoid impulse buying. He tracked every expense in a notebook and maintained a $500 emergency fund to avoid using credit for unexpected costs. When his phone broke, instead of using a credit card, he used his emergency fund and then developed a plan to replenish it over three months. This approach helped him avoid falling into debt while building strong financial habits.

Key Takeaways:

- Recognize types of debt: good vs. bad.
- Avoid debt traps through budgeting and saving.
- Use credit cards responsibly; pay balances monthly.
- Understand interest rates and their impact.
- Maintain good credit by timely repayments.

CHAPTER 8

INTRODUCTION TO INVESTING: MAKING YOUR MONEY GROW

Basic Principles of Investing

ONE WAY TO HELP your money grow is by investing. This means putting your money into things that might increase in value over time. Instead of just saving money in a piggy bank or a basic savings account, investing can offer a chance for bigger growth.

When you invest, you're buying something you believe will be worth more in the future. This could be shares of a company, bonds, or other assets. The idea is to put your money into something that can earn more money over time.

Starting early can make a big difference. Even small amounts of money can grow a lot over many years. This happens because of something called compound interest. Compound interest is when you earn interest not only on the money you put in but also on the interest it has already earned. Over time, this can make your money grow faster.

For example, if you invest $100 and it earns 5% interest each year, after the first year, you'll have $105. The next year, you earn interest on $105, not just the original $100. This means you'll earn more each year as your investment grows.

Diversifying your investments is also important. This means not putting all your money into one place. By spreading your money across different types of investments, you reduce the risk of losing it all if one investment doesn't do well.

Setting clear goals can help you make better investment choices. Think about what you want to achieve. Are you saving for college, a car, or something else? Knowing your goals will help you decide how much risk you're willing to take.

It's also important to understand the difference between saving and investing. Saving usually means putting money aside in a safe place, like a bank account, where it earns a small amount of interest. Investing involves more risk but can offer higher returns.

Learning about different types of investments can help you make informed decisions. Stocks, bonds, and mutual funds are common options. Each one works differently and has its own level of risk and potential return.

Remember that all investments come with some risk. There's no guarantee that you'll make money, and you could lose some or all of what you invest. That's why it's important to do your research and maybe talk to someone who knows about investing.

Patience is key when it comes to investing. Often, it takes time to see significant growth. Trying to get rich quick can lead to mistakes and losses.

Keep track of your investments and review them regularly. This doesn't mean checking them every day, but it's good to see how they're doing from time to time. This way, you can make changes if needed.

Starting to invest doesn't have to be complicated. There are many resources available to help beginners. You can read books, use online tools, or even start with investment apps designed for young people.

Learning with The Stock Market Game

1. **Visit The Stock Market Game: Go to www.stockmarketgame.org.**
2. **Click 'Register'**: Begin the registration process.
3. **Select 'Student'**: Indicate that you're a student participant.
4. **Provide School Information**: Enter details about your school if required.
5. **Get Approval**: Obtain necessary permissions from a teacher or guardian.
6. **Receive Login Credentials**: Check your email for account information.
7. **Log In**: Access your account on the platform.
8. **Start with Tutorials**: Complete any available tutorials on investing basics.
9. **Build a Portfolio**: Use virtual money to invest in stocks and other securities.
10. **Monitor Investments**: Track performance and learn from real-time market movements.
11. **Participate in Contests**: Join competitions, if available, to test your skills.

Understanding Risk and Return

Putting your money into investments comes with the chance of making more money, but it also comes with risks. Risk is the chance that you might lose some or all of the money you invest. Return is how much money you might make from your investment. Understanding how these two work together is important.

Every investment has a different level of risk and potential return. Usually, higher-risk investments can offer higher returns, but they also come with a greater chance of losing money. Lower-risk investments are safer, but they might not make as much money.

For example, putting money in a savings account is low risk. Your money is safe, but the interest you earn is small. Investing in stocks can offer higher returns, but there's a bigger chance you could lose money if the stock price goes down.

It's important to find a balance that works for you. Think about how much risk you're comfortable with. If losing money would make you very upset, you might want to choose safer investments. If you're okay with taking some risk for the chance of higher returns, you might choose different investments.

Time also plays a role in risk and return. If you're investing for a long time, you might be able to handle more risk because you have time to recover from any losses. If you only have a short time, you might want to choose safer investments.

Diversifying your investments can help manage risk. This means spreading your money across different types of investments. If one investment doesn't do well, others might do better, which can balance things out.

Understanding the risks of each investment helps you make better choices. Before investing, learn about what could go wrong and how likely that is. This way, you won't be surprised if things don't go as planned.

It's also helpful to set clear goals. Knowing what you want to achieve can guide your investment choices. If you're saving for something far in the future, you might choose different investments than if you need the money soon.

Talking to someone who knows about investing can provide important insights as you make decisions about your money. They can explain the risks and returns of different investment options and help you make decisions that are right for you.

Remember that no investment is completely without risk. Even the safest investments have some chance of not performing as expected. Being aware of this helps you be prepared for whatever happens.

Keeping an eye on your investments is important too. This doesn't mean worrying about every small change, but it's good to check in and see how things are going. If something isn't working out, you might decide to make changes.

Using Yahoo Finance for Investment Research

1. **Visit Yahoo Finance: Go to finance.yahoo.com.**
2. **Create an Account**: Sign up for free to customize your experience.
3. **Explore Market Data**: View real-time stock quotes and market summaries.
4. **Research Companies**: Use the search bar to find information on specific stocks.
5. **Read Analyst Reports**: Access professional analyses and opinions.
6. **Use Interactive Charts**: Examine historical performance of investments.
7. **Learn with Educational Articles**: Read content on investing strategies and terminology.
8. **Set Up Watchlists**: Add stocks to your watchlist to monitor them easily.
9. **Understand Risk Metrics**: Review indicators like beta and volatility for risk assessment.
10. **Stay Updated**: Follow financial news to keep informed about market trends.

Exercises:

1. **Compound Interest Calculation**: If you invest $1,000 at an annual interest rate of 5% compounded yearly, calculate the total amount after 5 years.
2. **Risk vs. Return Chart**: Create a chart comparing the risk and potential return of different investment types: savings accounts, bonds, stocks, and mutual funds.
3. **Investment Portfolio Project**: Design a simple investment portfolio with $2,000, allocating funds to various investment options based on your risk tolerance.
4. **Investment Goals Setting**: List three personal financial goals and explain how investing can help you achieve them over time.
5. **Diversification Illustration**: Explain the concept of diversification by providing examples of how investing in different assets can reduce risk.
6. **Investment Terminology Match**: Match the following terms with their definitions: Stocks, Bonds, Mutual Funds, Diversification, Compound Interest.

Case Studies

Phoenix's Investment Journey

Phoenix started investing at age 15 with $500 from summer jobs. Instead of keeping it in a regular savings account earning 0.5% interest, she researched different options. After learning about compound interest, she invested in a diversified mutual fund through a custodial account managed by her parents. The fund averaged 7% annual returns. She continued adding $50 monthly from her allowance. By age 18, her initial $500 had grown to $2,800, teaching her the power of starting early and compound interest. When the market experienced a temporary downturn, she stayed calm and maintained her regular investments, understanding that long-term growth was more important than short-term fluctuations.

Axel's Risk Management Lesson

Axel received $1,000 for his 16th birthday and decided to invest it all in a single tech company's stock because he liked their products. Within two months, the stock dropped 40% due to disappointing earnings reports. This experience taught him about the importance of diversification. He researched more and restructured his remaining money, splitting it between a low-cost index fund (60%), bonds (30%), and a high-interest savings account (10%). Over the next year, while some investments declined, others grew, resulting in a more stable overall portfolio that grew by 5% despite market volatility.

Tin's Goal-Based Investment Plan

Tin wanted to save $5,000 for specialized art equipment by age 19, giving her three years to invest. She developed a balanced strategy, putting 40% in a conservative bond fund, 40% in a stock market index fund, and keeping 20% in a high-yield savings account. She added $75 monthly from her part-time job. When art supplies went on sale, she resisted the urge to withdraw her investments early, understanding that frequent buying and selling could reduce her returns. Her patience paid off - her investments grew to $5,400, exceeding her goal through consistent contributions and a diversified approach.

Key Takeaways:

- Investing grows money over time.
- Start early to harness compound interest.
- Balance risk and return; diversify investments.
- Set clear investment goals.
- Understand basic investment principles.

CHAPTER 9

NEW MONEY CONCEPTS - CRYPTO AND AI

Cryptocurrency and Future Trends

MONEY ISN'T ALWAYS COINS or bills anymore; it can exist digitally on your phone or computer. This is the modern world of cryptocurrency. Cryptocurrencies are digital currencies that use cryptography for security. Unlike traditional money, they aren't controlled by any government or bank.

Bitcoin was the first cryptocurrency, created in 2009. It started as an idea to make transactions without using banks as middlemen. Now, thousands of cryptocurrencies exist, each with unique features. Some popular ones include Ethereum, Litecoin, and Ripple.

You might wonder how cryptocurrencies work. They use a technology called blockchain. Think of blockchain as a digital ledger or notebook that records all transactions. Once information is added, it can't be changed. This makes transactions secure and transparent.

Cryptocurrencies can be used to buy goods and services. Some online stores accept them as payment. They can also be traded for profit, similar to stocks. People buy them when prices are low and sell when prices rise.

The value of cryptocurrencies can change quickly. One day, the price might be high; the next day, it could drop. This is called volatility. It's important to be cautious and not invest money you can't afford to lose.

In the future, cryptocurrencies might become more common. Some experts believe they could change how we think about money. New types of cryptocurrencies are being developed with better technology and more features.

Decentralized finance, or DeFi, is another trend. It uses blockchain technology to offer financial services without banks. This means you could borrow, lend, or earn interest without needing a traditional bank account.

Digital currencies issued by governments, called Central Bank Digital Currencies (CB-DCs), are also being explored. Countries are looking into creating their own digital currencies to make transactions faster and more secure.

Non-fungible tokens, or NFTs, are another development in the crypto world. NFTs are unique digital items that can represent art, music, or virtual real estate. Owning an NFT means you have a one-of-a-kind digital asset.

Mining is a process where new cryptocurrency coins are created. People use powerful computers to solve complex math problems. When they solve these problems, they earn new coins as a reward. However, mining uses a lot of electricity, which can be bad for the environment. Because of this, some new cryptocurrencies are finding ways to be more eco-friendly.

Cryptocurrencies also face challenges. Since they're digital, they can be targets for hackers. Keeping your digital wallet secure is important. This means using strong passwords and being careful where you store your coins.

Regulation is another issue. Governments are still figuring out how to manage cryptocurrencies. Laws can vary from country to country, which can affect how cryptocurrencies are used.

Education is key. Learning about how cryptocurrencies work can help you avoid scams. Some people might try to trick others into investing in fake coins. Always do thorough research before making any investments.

The world of cryptocurrency is exciting and full of possibilities. As a teen, understanding these new money concepts can prepare you for the future. Technology is changing fast, and being informed can give you an advantage.

Exploring Cryptocurrency with Binance Academy

1. **Visit Binance Academy: Go to academy.binance.com.**
2. **Select Language**: Choose your preferred language from the dropdown menu.
3. **Navigate to 'Blockchain' Section**: Click on "Blockchain" to start learning basics.
4. **Read 'What is Cryptocurrency?'**: Begin with foundational articles.
5. **Watch Video Tutorials**: Engage with videos explaining complex concepts simply.
6. **Explore 'Crypto Safety'**: Learn about keeping your digital assets secure.
7. **Take Quizzes**: Test your knowledge after each module.
8. **Use Glossary**: Refer to the glossary for definitions of unfamiliar terms.
9. **Stay Informed**: Check the "Latest Articles" section for new developments.
10. **Join the Community**: Participate in forums or discussions if available.

How to Engage with AI as a Financial Tool

Artificial Intelligence, or AI, is changing the way we handle money. AI refers to computer systems that can perform tasks that usually require human intelligence. In finance, AI can help make smart decisions, manage money, and predict market trends.

One way AI is used in finance is through budgeting apps. These apps can track your spending and help you save money. By analyzing your habits, they suggest ways to cut costs and reach your financial goals.

Investment platforms also use AI. They can analyze vast amounts of data to find good investment opportunities. Some apps can create a personalized investment plan based on your risk level and financial goals.

Chatbots are another example. They have the ability to answer questions about your bank account or help you make transactions. This makes banking services available anytime, without waiting for a human representative.

AI can also help detect fraud. By monitoring transactions, AI systems are able to spot unusual activity. If something looks suspicious, they will alert you or your bank to prevent theft.

As a teen, you have access to AI tools that teach you about finance. Educational apps offer lessons on budgeting, investing, and saving, making learning interactive and fun.

When using AI tools, it's important to understand how they work. Knowing what data they collect and how they use it helps you stay informed. Always read the privacy policies and make sure your information is secure.

Setting up a budgeting app can be a good first step. By connecting your bank account, the app will be able to track your expenses. This makes it easier for you to set spending limits and savings goals. The app can send alerts when you're close to your limit or when you've reached a goal.

If you're interested in investing, some platforms offer simulated trading. This means you can practice investing with virtual money. It's a safe way to learn without risking real money.

Voice assistants like Siri or Alexa can also help. This makes managing money more convenient by having them check your account balance or set reminders to pay bills.

AI is also used in the stock market. High-frequency trading uses AI algorithms to make quick trades. While this is more advanced, understanding it gives you better insight into how modern markets operate.

Being aware of AI tools can prepare you for the future. As technology continues to grow, more financial services will use AI. Learning how to use these tools now might just give you an advantage later.

AI can also help you with financial planning. Some apps use AI to forecast your future expenses and income. By analyzing patterns, they can predict how much money you'll have in the future. This can help you plan for big purchases or saving for college.

Robo-advisors are another AI tool. They provide automated investment advice without needing a human advisor. By answering a few questions about your goals, the robo-advisor is then able to suggest an investment portfolio for you.

Learning about AI in finance could also open career opportunities. If you're interested in technology and money, fields like fintech might be exciting paths to explore for future careers.

Understanding risks is important too. AI systems are only as good as the data they use. Sometimes, they might make mistakes or not account for unexpected events. It's important to not rely entirely on AI and to use your own judgment.

Cybersecurity is a concern with AI tools. Since they often connect to your financial accounts, making sure they are secure is vital. Use strong passwords and enable two-factor authentication when possible.

Privacy is another aspect to consider. AI apps collect data to function effectively. Knowing how your data is used and stored helps protect your privacy. Always be extremely cautious with your personal information. Only use trusted apps and platforms. Protecting your data is important in keeping your finances secure.

You can also use AI to set financial reminders. Apps can notify you when bills are due or when it's time to review your budget. This helps you stay organized and avoid late fees.

Parents and guardians can use AI tools to teach teens about money. Some apps allow for shared accounts where both can track spending and savings. This encourages open discussions about financial habits.

Managing Finances with Emma – Your Best Financial Friend

1. **Download Emma App: Install from here.**
2. **Create an Account**: Sign up using your email and set a secure password.
3. **Link Financial Accounts**: Securely connect your bank accounts and credit cards.
4. **Set Up a Budget**: Use Emma's tools to create a personalized budget.
5. **Track Subscriptions**: Let Emma identify and monitor recurring payments.
6. **Receive Insights**: Get AI-generated tips on how to save money.
7. **Set Savings Goals**: Define financial goals and track progress within the app.
8. **Enable Notifications**: Stay updated on account activity and spending alerts.
9. **Use Spending Reports**: Analyze your spending habits with detailed reports.
10. **Engage with Support**: Access customer support for any questions or issues.

Challenges and Traps, Tips and Tricks

One challenge is the risk of scams. Some people create fake cryptocurrencies or investment opportunities to trick others. Always research thoroughly before investing in anything. Look for information from trusted sources.

The volatility of cryptocurrencies is another concern. Prices can change rapidly, and it's possible to lose money quickly. It's important to only invest what you can afford to lose.

Security is a big issue. Hackers might try to steal your digital assets. Keeping your digital wallets and accounts secure is essential. Use strong, unique passwords and consider using hardware wallets for cryptocurrencies.

Understanding the technology can be difficult. Concepts like blockchain and AI are complex. Taking the time to learn and ask questions helps you make better decisions.

When using AI tools, be aware of data privacy. Some apps might collect more information than you're comfortable sharing. Read privacy policies and understand what data is being collected.

Over-reliance on AI can be a trap. While AI is often able to provide helpful insights, it's important to ultimately use your own judgment. Don't let an app make all your financial decisions without considering them yourself.

Now, let's look at some tips and tricks to help you navigate these new money concepts.

Educate yourself. Knowledge is power. Read books, watch videos, and take online courses to understand cryptocurrencies and AI.

Use small amounts at first. If you're interested in investing, start with a small amount of money. This way, you can learn effectively without risking too much.

Use trusted platforms. Only use well-known apps and websites for trading and managing your money. Check reviews and ask others for recommendations.

Keep your software updated. Updates often include security patches that protect you from new threats. Regularly updating your apps and devices will keep your information safer.

Set up two-factor authentication. This adds an extra layer of security to your accounts. Even if someone knows your password, they won't be able to access your account without the second form of verification.

Be cautious of too-good-to-be-true offers. If someone promises high returns with little or no risk, it might be a scam. Always be skeptical of unrealistic promises.

Diversify your investments. Don't put all your money into one cryptocurrency or investment. Spreading out your investments can reduce risk.

Stay updated on news and trends. The world of crypto and AI is constantly changing. Following reputable news sources can help you stay informed.

Connect with communities. Online forums and groups are a great place to learn from others. Just be cautious and verify the information you receive.

Practice good digital hygiene. Be careful about what you click on and download. Avoid phishing emails and suspicious links that could compromise your security.

Ask for advice. Talk to parents, teachers, or financial advisors if you're unsure about something. Getting input from trusted adults helps you make better choices.

Exercises:

1. **Cryptocurrency Research**: Choose a cryptocurrency (e.g., Bitcoin, Ethereum) and write a summary of how it works and its potential uses.
2. **Blockchain Diagram**: Create a simple diagram illustrating how blockchain technology secures transactions.
3. **AI Financial Tool Exploration**: Find an AI-powered budgeting app and list its features. Discuss how AI improves personal finance management.
4. **Security Plan Development**: Outline steps to secure digital assets like cryptocurrencies, including wallet types and safety practices.
5. **Pros and Cons List**: List three advantages and three disadvantages of using cryptocurrencies in everyday transactions.

6. **Current Trends Essay**: Write a short essay on how AI is shaping the future of finance and what it means for personal money management.

Case Studies

Cryptocurrency in Cross-Border Payments

Elena is a freelance web developer who has clients all over the world. She often struggled with the high fees and long processing times associated with international wire transfers when receiving payments. After learning about cryptocurrencies, she started accepting Bitcoin from her overseas clients. The transactions are fast, cheap, and she can access her earnings immediately. This has improved her cash flow and made it easier to manage her global client base.

Budgeting with AI

Juan is a high school student who wants to save up for a new laptop. He downloaded a popular budgeting app that uses AI to track his spending. The app automatically categorizes his purchases and provides insights on where he can cut back. It also helped him set a savings goal and sent alerts when he was nearing his limit for discretionary spending. Using the app, Juan was able to save the full amount for the laptop in just 6 months.

Robo-Advisor for College Investing

Tyra is a junior in high school and is starting to think about saving for college. She signed up for a robo-advisor service that recommended an investment portfolio based on her time horizon and risk tolerance. The robo-advisor automatically rebalances the portfolio and reinvests dividends. Tyra doesn't have to actively manage the investments, allowing her to focus on her studies while still growing her college fund.

Key Takeaways:

- Cryptocurrencies use blockchain for secure transactions.
- AI enhances financial decision-making.

- New technologies offer opportunities and risks.
- Stay informed and cautious with crypto and AI.
- Protect digital assets and personal data.

CHAPTER 10

PRACTICAL TIPS FOR FINANCIAL INDEPENDENCE

Handling Unexpected Expenses

UNEXPECTED COSTS CAN POP up when you least expect them. Maybe your bike needs a repair, or your phone screen cracks. These situations can be stressful if you're not prepared.

Saving a little money regularly is a great way to help you deal with surprise expenses. Setting aside even a small amount each time you receive money will add up over time. This is often called an emergency fund.

For example, putting away a few dollars each week can make a big difference. After several months, these savings grow, and you'll have funds ready when an unexpected cost arises.

Thinking ahead about possible surprise expenses is also helpful. Do you have hobbies that might require new equipment? Are there school activities that might cost extra money? By considering these possibilities, you become better prepared to handle anything that might come up.

Keeping track of where your money goes is another good idea. Write down your daily spending to see patterns and help you find areas where you can save more. Maybe skipping a snack purchase can add to your savings.

It's important to keep your emergency savings separate from your spending money. While it might be tempting to use these funds for fun things, try to resist. This money is meant to help when unexpected costs arise. And unexpected costs do indeed arise!

If you face an unexpected expense and don't have enough saved, consider ways to earn extra money. You could offer to do chores for neighbors, tutor younger students, or sell items you no longer need.

Don't hesitate to talk to your family about financial surprises. They might offer advice or help you come up with solutions. Sharing your concerns can make the situation less stressful.

Creating a simple budget is an important way to assist in managing your money. Decide how much you'll save and how much you'll spend each week or month. This plan is a good way to help you stay on track with your financial goals.

Looking for discounts and sales is yet another way to help you save money. When you need to buy something, check if it's on sale or if there's a less expensive option. This way, you spend less and save more.

Taking good care of your belongings prevents some unexpected expenses. If you keep your things in good condition, they last longer, and you won't need to replace them as often.

Learning to fix small problems yourself can save money too. If a button falls off your shirt, sewing it back on instead of buying a new shirt keeps money in your pocket. These small skills are ways to help avoid extra costs.

Protecting Yourself from Financial Scams

It's important to be careful with your money. Sometimes, people try to trick others into giving away their money or personal information. These tricks are called scams.

One common scam is when someone offers a deal that sounds too good to be true. They might promise a lot of money for doing very little work. Be cautious if someone you don't know offers quick and easy money.

Never share any personal information with strangers. This includes bank account details, passwords, or even your home address. Scammers can use this information to steal money or pretend to be you.

Be careful when you're online. If you get an email or message asking for personal information, don't reply unless you're absolutely sure it's safe. Scammers often send messages that look real but are fake. When in doubt, contact the sender of the message directly and don’t reply to the message in question.

If you see a website or online ad that offers free things in exchange for your information, think twice. These can be traps to collect your details. Always check with a trusted adult before sharing any information online.

Sometimes, scammers might pretend to be someone you know. They could send a message saying they're a friend and need money. If this happens, try to contact your friend in another way to make sure it's really them.

At school, you might hear about cyber safety. Following these rules can help protect you from scams. Being careful online is just as important as being careful in person.

If someone pressures you to make a quick decision about money, be careful. Scammers often try to rush people so they don't have time to think. Take your time and talk to someone you trust before making any decisions.

Never agree to send money to someone you don't know. Even if they promise to pay you back or give you more money later, it's risky. It's better to be safe and hold on to your money.

If you're unsure about a situation, ask a parent, teacher, or another trusted adult. They can help you figure out if something is a scam.

Remember that real businesses won't ask for passwords or personal details over email or text. If you get a message like this, it's likely a scam. When in doubt, always contact the company directly in another way to make sure you are actually communicating with that specific company.

Being careful with your money and information helps keep you safe. Learning to spot scams is an important skill. The more you know, the better you will be able to protect yourself.

There are many types of scams to watch out for. Some might offer a prize or scholarship that you didn't apply for. If you receive a message saying you've won something but need to pay a fee to claim it, be cautious. Remember that when it seems "too good to be true," it usually is.

Another scam targets people selling items online. If you're selling something and the buyer wants to overpay with a check and asks to send back the extra money, it could be a trick. The check might be fake, and you'll lose the money you sent back.

On social media, scammers might create fake accounts pretending to be celebrities or influencers. They might ask you to click on links or enter contests. Be careful and verify if the account is real before interacting.

Protecting your passwords is very important. Use strong passwords that are hard to guess. Don't use the same password for everything. Changing your passwords regularly can also help keep your accounts safe.

When using public computers or Wi-Fi, be extra careful. Public access is not very secure at all. Protect yourself online! Avoid logging into important accounts on public networks, as others might be able to see your information.

Keep your computer and devices updated with the latest security software. This helps protect you from viruses and hackers who might try to steal your information.

If you think you've been scammed, don't be afraid to tell someone. The sooner you report it, the better chance you have of fixing the problem. You can talk to a parent, teacher, or even the police if needed.

Educate yourself about common scams. The more you know, the better you can spot them. There are websites and resources that teach about scams and how to avoid them.

Being careful doesn't mean you have to be scared. It's about being smart and making good choices. Trustworthy businesses and people will understand if you need time to think or ask questions.

Your personal information is valuable. Protecting it helps keep you and your money safe. Stay informed, be cautious, and don't hesitate to seek help when needed.

Staying Safe with OnGuardOnline.gov

1. **Visit OnGuardOnline.gov**: Go to www.consumer.ftc.gov/features/feature-0038-onguardonline.
2. **Explore Topics**: Browse sections like "Phishing," "Identity Theft," and "Online Shopping."
3. **Watch Videos**: View educational videos on avoiding scams.
4. **Read Articles**: Gain insights from articles about online safety.
5. **Take Quizzes**: Test your knowledge with interactive quizzes.
6. **Download Materials**: Access free brochures and guides.
7. **Sign Up for Alerts**: Subscribe to receive updates on new scams.
8. **Report Scams**: Learn how to report suspicious activities.
9. **Share with Others**: Educate friends and family about staying safe.
10. **Stay Informed**: Regularly check the site for new information.

Developing Good Financial Habits for Life

Sow the seeds of healthy money habits now, and you'll reap the harvest of financial security for years to come. Every decision you make today sets the foundation for a strong financial future.

Saving regularly is an important habit. Even if it's just a small amount, putting money aside now can allow it the opportunity to grow over time. This teaches discipline and prepares you for future needs.

Understanding the difference between wants and needs is also key. Needs are things you must have, like food and clothes. Wants are things you'd like to have but can live without. Learning to prioritize needs helps make better spending choices.

Creating a budget is a useful tool. A budget helps plan how to use money wisely. You can write down how much money you have and decide how much to spend and save.

Being mindful of spending is another good habit. Before buying something, ask yourself if it's really needed. Waiting a day or two before making a purchase will help you decide whether it's truly important or whether it can wait. Delaying gratification is a wise tactic in responsible money management.

Chart your course to financial well-being by gathering information from reliable guides. Tap into the knowledge of parents and teachers, or dive into the world of finance through insightful books.. The more you know, the better you will be able to manage your money.

Avoiding debt is important. Borrowing money might seem like a quick solution, but it can lead to big problems if you find yourself unable to pay it back. Try to use the money you have instead of relying on others.

Keeping track of money helps you see where it goes. Use a notebook or an app to record spending and savings. Staying organized and aware will allow you to reach your goals.

Practicing generosity is also valuable. Sharing with others or donating to causes you care about can bring joy and make a difference. It teaches us the value of helping and not just receiving.

Being patient with financial progress is important. Saving money and reaching goals takes time. Celebrate small achievements along the way to stay motivated.

Mistakes happen! If you discover that you've spent more than planned or forgotten to save, don't be too hard on yourself. Learn from these experiences and work on building awareness and doing better next time.

Understanding how interest works is the key to growing your wealth. When you save money in a bank account, you're not just keeping it safe - you're putting it to work! If you keep your money in a savings account, you might earn interest. t. This means the bank pays a little extra money for keeping savings there. Over time, this can really add up.

Starting good habits early gives you a big advantage. The earlier you begin saving and managing money effectively, the more it can grow. This will help you reach bigger goals in the future.

It's also helpful to learn about different ways of saving and investing money. While some options might only be available to adults, knowing about them now will help you prepare for later.

Ask questions whenever you are unsure. No one expects you to know everything about money right away. Seeking advice from trusted sources demonstrates responsibility and a willingness to learn.

Being honest with yourself about finances is important. If you know you have trouble saving, think about why and how to improve. Maybe set up automatic savings or find ways to reduce spending.

Stay open to learning new things. The world of money changes all the time, and there's always more to discover. Keeping up with these changes will put you in a position to make the best possible decisions.

Building Habits with Fabulous Daily Motivation

1. **Download Fabulous App: Install from here.**
2. **Create an Account**: Sign up using your email or social media accounts.
3. **Set Your Journey**: Choose "Build Healthy Habits" as your main goal.
4. **Add Financial Habits**: Input habits like "Save $5 daily" or "Track expenses."
5. **Schedule Routines**: Set times for when you'll perform each habit.
6. **Receive Reminders**: Enable notifications to keep you on track.
7. **Reflect Daily**: Use the app's journal feature to note progress and challenges.
8. **Access Coaching Sessions**: Listen to motivational content for support.
9. **Track Progress**: View streaks and achievements within the app.
10. **Adjust as Needed**: Modify habits and routines to fit your lifestyle.

Exercises:

1. **Emergency Fund Calculation**: Determine how much you should have in an emergency fund to cover three months of expenses. Create a savings plan to reach that goal.
2. **Scam Awareness Quiz**: Develop a quiz with five questions to test knowledge on identifying financial scams.
3. **Habit Evaluation**: List your current financial habits. Identify two positive

habits to continue and two negative habits to improve.

4. **Monthly Expense Tracker**: Track all your expenses for a month to identify areas where you can reduce spending and increase savings.
5. **Financial Goals Worksheet**: Set SMART (Specific, Measurable, Achievable, Relevant, Time-bound) financial goals for the next year.
6. **Role-Play Scenario**: Practice responding to a phishing email or scam call. Write out your response that protects your information.

Case Studies

Raven's Emergency Preparedness

Raven's skateboard was her main transportation to work at the local cafe. When it broke unexpectedly, she needed $150 for repairs. Fortunately, she had been saving $10 weekly from her cafe tips in a separate emergency fund. Initially, saving felt difficult, but she made it automatic by putting aside money right after each shift. When her skateboard broke, she had $200 saved. After paying for repairs, she immediately began rebuilding her emergency fund, setting a new goal of $300 to prepare for future unexpected expenses.

Storm's Scam Avoidance

Storm received a text message claiming he won a $1,000 gaming system in a contest he never entered. The message asked him to click a link and provide his address and bank information to claim the prize. Though excited, he remembered learning about scams in school. Instead of clicking, he showed the message to his parents. They discovered it was a phishing scam targeting teenagers. Storm blocked the number and shared his experience with friends, helping them recognize similar scam attempts.

Cypress's Habit Formation

Cypress struggled with impulsive spending until she created a system to build better financial habits. She started by waiting 24 hours before any purchase over $20. She tracked daily expenses in a small notebook and reviewed them weekly. To make saving easier, she labeled three jars: "Needs," "Wants," and "Future." Each time she received money, she split it between the jars before spending any. After six months, these habits became automatic. Her "Future" jar contained $340, which she used to buy art supplies for her small business instead of borrowing money.

Key Takeaways:

- Build an emergency fund for surprises.
- Stay vigilant against financial scams.
- Cultivate lifelong good financial habits.
- Regularly set and review financial goals.
- Wise management leads to independence.

Conclusion

Over the past chapters, we've explored many ideas to help you handle money wisely. Starting with the basics, we learned how to create a simple budget. This helps you keep track of what you earn and what you spend, so you can save money for things that matter to you. We practiced making a budget by listing all income sources, like allowance or part-time jobs, and all expenses, such as snacks, games, or clothes.

We also talked about different types of bank accounts. Knowing the difference between checking and savings accounts can help you decide where you want to keep your money. A checking account is good for everyday spending, while a savings account is better for the long term, keeping your money safe and earning a bit of interest over time. We discussed how to use a debit card and the importance of keeping personal information safe. Remember to never share your PIN with anyone.

Credit cards can be tricky, but we learned how they work and why it's important to pay them off each month. Using a credit card wisely can help you build good credit, which will help you later when you want to buy a car or even a house. We also learned about the dangers of debt and how interest can make you owe more money over time. The information shared here is intended to help you avoid getting trapped.

Investing was another big topic. We talked about stocks, bonds, and mutual funds. By starting to invest early, even with small amounts, you can watch your money grow over time. We learned that investing is a way to make your money work for you, but it also comes with risks. It's important to research and maybe talk to a trusted adult before investing.

We also explored newer kinds of money, like Bitcoin and other cryptocurrencies. While they can be exciting, they also come with risks. It's crucial to learn as much as you can before investing in them. Cryptocurrencies can go up and down in value very quickly, so understanding how they work is key.

Understanding taxes is important too. We learned about why we pay taxes and how to file a simple tax return. Taxes help pay for things like schools, roads, and parks. Knowing this can help you avoid problems and maybe even get some money back. We also talked about ways to keep good records so that filing taxes becomes easier.

Along the way, we shared tips on how to earn extra money. From doing chores to starting a small business like mowing lawns or babysitting, there are many ways to increase your income. We also talked about the importance of hard work and creativity in making money. Thinking outside the box can lead to new opportunities.

Protecting your money is just as important as earning it. We talked about the importance of insurance and how it can help you if something unexpected happens. For example, health insurance can help pay for doctor visits, and car insurance can help if you're in an accident. Understanding these protections can save you from big costs later on.

Learning about money doesn't stop here. The more you use what you've learned, the better you'll get at making smart choices. Every day brings new chances to practice good habits, like saving a part of your allowance or thinking carefully before buying something.

Making a budget and sticking to it might seem hard at first, but over time, it becomes easier. Try to write down what you spend for a week or a month. This can help you see where your money goes and find ways to save more. Maybe you'll notice that small expenses add up, and you can decide to cut back on things that aren't important.

Remember, it's okay to make mistakes. Everyone does. The important thing is to learn from them. If you spend too much one week, think about how you can do better next time. Maybe you can pack a lunch instead of buying one, or wait for a sale before purchasing that game you want. Learning from your mistakes helps you make better choices in the future.

Don't forget to talk to others about money. Your parents, teachers, or a trusted adult can give you advice and answer your questions. Sometimes, they might share their own experiences and tips. They might tell you about times when they made good or bad money decisions, and what they learned from them.

Keep learning about new ways to manage and grow your money. There are always new things to discover, like apps that help you save or invest. Staying curious will allow you to you stay ahead. You might read articles, watch videos, or even take a class about money management.

Mastering your money now isn't just about today, it's about unlocking a world of future possibilities. The smart financial habits you build today can pave the way for big dreams like owning a car, going to college, or even starting your own business someday. Think of yourself as the driver of your own financial journey. Every choice you make puts you on a path toward your goals.

Also, consider sharing what you've learned with your friends. You can help each other make good choices and maybe even start a savings club or a small business together. Working with others can make learning more fun and keep you motivated.

You're not alone on this journey. Many people are learning how to manage money, just like you. Stay positive and keep working towards your goals. If you face challenges, don't give up. Look for solutions and keep moving forward.

Every step you take brings you closer to financial independence. Celebrate your successes, no matter how small. Saving a few dollars or choosing not to buy something unnecessary are victories. Recognizing these wins can boost your confidence.

Stay focused, keep learning, and believe in yourself. You've already come so far, and the future is full of possibilities. By continuing to apply what you've learned, you can build a bright and successful future for yourself.

Continuing your financial education is a great idea. There are many resources available to help you learn more and answer your questions. Spend some time investigating the resources shared in this book. They will help you along your path.

Your local library is a great place to start! You can find books about money management, investing, and starting a business. Librarians can help you find books that are easy to understand and interesting. Some libraries also offer free workshops or events where you can learn about money topics. Take advantage of these to bring your money management game to the next level.

There are also websites specifically designed to help teens learn about money. Websites like MoneySense and Practical Money Skills offer games, articles, and quizzes that make learning fun. These sites cover topics like saving, budgeting, and even understanding the stock market. Another site, Jump$tart Coalition, provides resources to help young people get smart about personal finance.

Many apps can help you manage your money. Apps like Mint or YNAB (You Need A Budget) can help you track your spending and savings. Some apps even have features that teach you about investing or setting savings goals. Acorns is an app that helps you start investing with small amounts, like spare change from purchases.

Consider talking to your school's guidance counselor or teachers. They might know of clubs, classes, or programs that focus on financial literacy. Joining a club can help you meet others who are interested in learning about money. Some schools offer classes on economics or personal finance that you might be able to take.

Some banks offer programs for young people. They might have workshops or online courses that teach you how to manage your accounts, use online banking safely, or start investing. Don't be afraid to ask at your local bank branch. They might even offer special accounts for teens with lower fees or other benefits.

There are also plenty of videos and podcasts that can help you learn. Channels like Crash Course Economics on YouTube explain financial concepts in a way that's easy to understand. Podcasts like "Planet Money" discuss money topics in a fun way. Listening to these can make learning about money more enjoyable.

If you're interested in investing, there are simulations like Stock Market Game where you can practice buying and selling stocks without using real money. This can help you learn how the stock market works without any risk. Another simulation is the Investopedia Stock Simulator, which also allows you to practice trading.

Your parents or guardians can be a great resource too. Ask them questions about how they manage money, pay bills, or save for big expenses. They might share valuable lessons they've learned over the years. Sometimes, having regular family meetings to talk about money can help everyone learn together.

Community centers or local organizations sometimes offer workshops or classes for teens. These can be a great way to learn and meet new people. Check bulletin boards or community calendars to see what's available in your area.

Books written specifically for teens can be very helpful. Titles like "The Teen's Guide to Personal Finance" or "A Smart Girl's Guide: Money" are written in a way that's easy to read and relate to. Reading different books can give you new ideas and perspectives.

Online forums or groups can also provide support. Be sure to stay safe online by not sharing personal information and only using trusted sites. Websites like Reddit have communities where people share tips and ask questions about money.

Continuing to learn and seek support will help you become even better at managing your money. The more you know, the more confident you'll feel in making decisions. Keep exploring new resources and don't hesitate to reach out when you have questions.

Your journey toward financial independence is unique and valuable. By sharing your own experiences and thoughts, you can inspire others who are starting on the same path.

Consider telling others about what you've learned and how it's made a difference in your life. You might have insights or tips that could help your friends, classmates, or even people you've never met. Sharing your story can motivate others to take control of their finances too.

Writing down your thoughts can also help you reflect on how far you've come. You might choose to write a journal entry, a blog post, or share on social media. Talking about your goals and achievements can make them feel even more real. It can also help you stay accountable and focused on your objectives.

There are places online where people discuss money management and share advice. Joining these communities can increase your learning and allow you to connect with others who have similar interests. You can ask questions, offer answers, and be part of a supportive group. Websites like financial forums or social media groups focused on teens and money can be great places to start.

If you have suggestions or ideas about how resources could be improved for teens learning about money, sharing your thoughts can help creators make better tools for everyone. Your feedback is valuable and can lead to positive changes. You might send an email, fill out a feedback form, or participate in surveys.

Some platforms allow you to leave reviews or ratings for resources you've used. This can help others decide if a particular tool or guide is right for them. By sharing your honest opinion, you're contributing to a community of learners. Your review might highlight what you found most helpful or suggest areas for improvement.

Perhaps you can encourage your school or local library to offer more resources on financial literacy. Sharing your positive experiences might motivate them to add more books, workshops, or programs that can help other teens. You could talk to a teacher, librarian, or school counselor about your interests.

Talking with your parents or guardians about what you've learned can also strengthen your relationships. They might be interested to hear about your goals and want to support you in achieving them. Maybe you can work together on family budgeting or discuss plans for your future education.

Your voice matters! By speaking up and sharing your journey, you're helping to build a community where everyone can learn and grow together. Your experiences can inspire others to take control of their finances and work toward their dreams.

Accessing Financial Literacy Resources on MoneySense

1. **Visit MoneySense**: Go to www.moneysense.ca.

2. **Navigate to 'Learn' Section**: Click on "Learn" in the top menu.

3. **Choose Topics of Interest**: Select areas like "Budgeting," "Saving," or "Investing."
4. **Read Expert Articles**: Access articles written by financial experts.
5. **Use Tools and Calculators**: Utilize online calculators for financial planning.
6. **Subscribe to Newsletter**: Sign up to receive regular financial tips.
7. **Download Guides**: Access free e-books and guides on personal finance.
8. **Watch Videos**: Engage with visual content for easier understanding.
9. **Participate in Quizzes**: Test your knowledge on various financial topics.
10. **Follow on Social Media**: Stay connected through their social media channels for updates.

Joining a Financial Community on Nextdoor

1. **Download Nextdoor App: Install from here.**
2. **Sign Up**: Register using your address to connect with your local community.
3. **Verify Your Address**: Follow instructions to confirm your location.
4. **Complete Your Profile**: Add a photo and brief bio.
5. **Join Local Groups**: Search for finance or teen groups in your area.
6. **Start a Discussion**: Post questions or share experiences about financial topics.
7. **Engage with Neighbors**: Comment on posts and offer support or advice.

8. **Attend Local Events**: Look for community meetings or workshops on finance.
9. **Create a Group**: If none exist, start your own group focused on teen finance.
10. **Stay Active**: Regularly participate to build connections and learn from others.

Exercises:

1. **Comprehensive Review Quiz**: Create a 10-question quiz covering key concepts from all of the previous chapters to test your understanding.
2. **Personal Finance Reflection**: Write a personal reflection on how your attitudes toward money have changed after studying this material.
3. **Resource Compilation**: Gather a list of helpful financial tools, apps, and websites for ongoing learning and support.
4. **Financial Advice Letter**: Write a letter to a younger sibling or friend giving them financial advice based on what you've learned.
5. **Action Plan Update**: Review and update your financial goals and action plans, incorporating new insights and strategies.
6. **Community Engagement**: Plan a way to share your financial knowledge with others, such as a workshop, blog, or school club.

Key Takeaways:

- Regular practice strengthens money management skills.
- Start with basic budgeting and build from there.
- Different account types serve different purposes.
- Investing early can help money grow over time.

- Insurance protects against unexpected losses.
- Keep learning through various resources and tools.

QR Codes Index

WWW.ETSY.COM

Chapter 1

https://www.irs.gov

Chapter 1

https://www.khanacademy.org

Chapter 2

https://www.trello.com

Chapter 2

https://www.practicalmoneyskills.com

Chapter 3

https://mint.intuit.com/

Chapter 3

https://pocketguard.com/

Chapter 4

https://www.wally.com/en-us/

Chapter 4

https://www.capitalone.com/bank/savings-accounts/kids-savings-account

Chapter 5

https://www.acorns.com/

Chapter 5

https://www.savingforcollege.com

Chapter 6

https://studentaid.gov

Chapter 6

https://www.undebt.it

Chapter 7

https://www.creditkarma.com

Chapter 7

https://www.stockmarketgame.org

Chapter 8

https://finance.yahoo.com

Chapter 8

https://academy.binance.com

Chapter 9

https://emma-app.com/

Chapter 9

https://www.consumer.ftc.gov/features/feature-0038-onguardonline

Chapter 10

https://www.thefabulous.co/

Chapter 10

https://sheets.google.com

Chapter 11

https://www.ngpf.org

Chapter 11

https://www.moneysense.ca

Conclusion

https://nextdoor.com/

Conclusion

Glossary

1. **Allowance**: Money given regularly, often by parents, that you can spend or save as you choose. Managing your allowance helps you learn about budgeting.

2. **Assets**: Items of value that you own. These include things like cash, a bicycle, a computer, or collectibles such as rare cards. Assets can help you in the future because you can sell them or they can generate income for you.

3. **ATM**: A machine that lets you withdraw or deposit money into your bank account using a card. ATMs are convenient for accessing cash when you need it.

4. **Bank Account**: An account at a bank where you can keep your money safe and access it when needed. Banks may offer interest on the money you keep with them.

5. **Bond**: A way to lend money to a company or government. They promise to pay you back later with extra money called interest. Bonds are considered less risky than stocks.

6. **Budget**: A simple plan that shows how you will spend and save your money. It helps ensure you don't run out of money and can reach your financial goals.

7. **Budget Deficit**: When you spend more money than you earn, leading to debt.

Avoiding deficits helps keep your finances healthy.

8. **Budget Surplus**: When you earn more money than you spend, allowing you to save or invest the extra. Surpluses help you build wealth over time.
9. **Budgeting App**: A tool on your phone or computer that helps you track where your money goes and how much you save. It makes managing your finances easier and more organized.
10. **Capital**: Money used to start or grow a business or make investments. Having capital is important for entrepreneurship and investing.
11. **Checking Account**: A bank account for daily spending. You can write checks or use a debit card to pay for things. It's useful for managing everyday expenses.
12. **Compound Interest**: Interest earned on interest. This helps your savings grow faster over time. For example, if you earn interest on $100, next time you earn interest on $100 plus the interest you already earned.
13. **Credit**: Borrowing money now with the promise to pay it back later. This can help you buy things you need but don't have the cash for right away. It's important to pay it back on time.
14. **Credit Card**: A card that lets you borrow money up to a limit to make purchases, which you pay back later. Responsible use builds a good credit history.
15. **Credit Score**: A number that shows how well you manage borrowed money. A higher score means you are good at paying back loans, which can help you get better interest rates.
16. **Cryptocurrency**: Digital money that exists only online. It uses special technology to keep it secure. Bitcoin is one type. Cryptocurrencies can be risky because their value can change quickly.
17. **Debit Card**: A card linked to your bank account that lets you spend money you have. It's a convenient way to pay without carrying cash.
18. **Debt**: Money you owe to others. This could be from borrowing money, using a credit card, or not paying bills on time.

19. **Diversification**: Not putting all your eggs in one basket. This means spreading your investments around so if one loses value, others might not. It helps reduce risk.

20. **Dividend**: Money paid to shareholders when a company shares its profits. Dividends provide income to investors.

21. **Emergency Fund**: Money saved for unexpected events like a broken phone or sudden expenses. Having this fund helps you avoid debt and stay financially secure.

22. **Entrepreneur**: A person who starts and runs their own business, taking on financial risks in hopes of making a profit.

23. **Equity**: The value of ownership in something, like a company or property, after subtracting any debts. Owning equity means having a stake in the asset.

24. **Expense**: Money you spend on things like food, clothes, games, or other activities. Keeping track of expenses helps you manage your money better.

25. **Financial Advisor**: A professional who helps you make decisions about saving, investing, and managing money. They can guide you toward your financial goals.

26. **Financial Goal**: Something you are saving money for, like a new bike, college, or starting a business. Setting goals helps you stay focused on saving and spending wisely.

27. **Financial Literacy**: Knowing how to manage money, including earning, saving, spending, and investing. Financial literacy helps you make smart decisions with your money.

28. **Gross Income**: All the money you earn before any taxes or other deductions are taken out. It's your total earnings from all sources.

29. **Identity Theft**: When someone steals your personal information to use your money or open accounts in your name. Protecting your information helps prevent this.

30. **Income**: Money you earn or receive. This can come from a job, allowance, or

gifts. Income is used to pay for expenses and can be saved for the future.

31. **Inflation**: When prices for things go up over time. This means money buys less than it used to, so you need more money to buy the same things.

32. **Inflation Rate**: The speed at which prices for goods and services increase over time. High inflation can reduce the buying power of your money.

33. **Insurance**: A way to protect yourself financially against unexpected events by paying a small amount regularly. Types include health, car, and property insurance.

34. **Interest**: Extra money paid for borrowing money or earned for saving money. If you borrow $100 with 5% interest, you pay back $105. When you save money, interest helps your savings grow.

35. **Interest Rate**: The percentage charged when you borrow money or earned when you save money. Higher interest rates mean more cost for loans or more earnings on savings.

36. **Investment**: Putting money into something with the hope that it will grow over time. This could be starting a small business, buying stocks, or finding other ways to make your money work for you.

37. **IRA**: An Individual Retirement Account. It lets you save money for retirement with tax advantages, even if your employer doesn't offer a plan.

38. **Liability**: An amount you owe or are responsible for paying back. Liabilities can reduce your net worth because they are debts that need to be paid.

39. **Liquidity**: How quickly and easily you can turn something you own into cash without losing value. Cash is the most liquid asset.

40. **Loan**: Money borrowed that must be paid back with interest over time. Loans can help you make big purchases but need to be managed carefully.

41. **Minimum Payment**: The smallest amount you must pay on your credit card bill to avoid penalties. Paying only the minimum can lead to more interest charges over time.

42. **Mortgage**: A loan used to buy a house, which is paid back over many years. The house is used as security for the loan.

43. **Mutual Fund**: A collection of many stocks or bonds, managed by experts. This lets you invest in lots of companies at once without buying each stock individually.

44. **Net Income**: The amount of money you actually take home after taxes and deductions. This is the money you can spend or save.

45. **Net Worth**: A simple way to see how much wealth you have. Subtract what you owe (liabilities) from what you own (assets). If you have $1,000 in assets and $300 in liabilities, your net worth is $700.

46. **Opportunity Cost**: The benefit you miss out on when choosing one option over another. For example, buying a game now means you can't save that money for something else later.

47. **Overdraft**: When you spend more money than you have in your bank account. This can result in fees and is important to avoid by tracking your balance.

48. **Passive Income**: Money you earn without actively working for it regularly, like from investments, rental properties, or royalties from creative work.

49. **Portfolio**: All your investments combined. This shows everything you own in stocks, bonds, or other assets and helps you see your overall financial picture.

50. **Principal**: The original sum of money invested or borrowed, not including interest or earnings. Paying down the principal reduces the amount of interest owed.

51. **Recession**: A time when the economy slows down, and many businesses make less money, leading to job losses. Understanding this can help you prepare financially.

52. **Return**: The money made or lost on an investment over a period of time. Returns can be positive or negative and are important for measuring investment performance.

53. **Retirement Account**: A special account where you save money for when you're older and stop working. Starting early helps your money grow over time.

54. **Risk**: The chance that an investment might lose money or not perform as expected. Understanding risk helps you make better investment choices.

55. **Savings**: Money you set aside to use in the future. This can help you pay for big things or emergencies without borrowing. Saving regularly helps you reach your financial goals.

56. **Savings Account**: An account where you can store money and earn interest over time. Savings accounts encourage you to save by keeping your money separate from dailyspending.

57. **Stock**: A small piece of a company that you can own. If the company does well, your stock might become more valuable, and you might earn money when you sell it.

58. **Stock Exchange**: A place where stocks are bought and sold. Companies list their stocks here so people can invest and trade.

59. **Tax**: Money you pay to the government to help fund public services like schools and roads. Taxes are taken from income, sales, and property.

60. **Time Value of Money**: The idea that money available now is worth more than the same amount in the future because it can earn interest. Saving early takes advantage of this.

61. **401(k)**: A retirement savings plan offered by some employers in the U.S. You can save money before taxes are taken out, and sometimes employers match your contributions.

About the Author

At the age of ten, Dianne Williams opened her first bank savings account. Her parents believed it was important for her to learn about money early. They encouraged her to save a part of her pocket money each week. This simple act taught her the value of saving and planning for the future. She began to set small goals, such as saving up for a new toy or a special treat. Watching her savings grow gave her a sense of accomplishment and responsibility. Sometimes, she helped with extra chores around the house to earn a bit more to add to her savings. These early experiences laid the foundation for her understanding of financial management.

In her mid-teens, Dianne started working after school as a checkout operator at a local store. This was her first real job, and she was excited to earn her own money. Handling cash and dealing with customers gave her valuable experience. She learned about responsibility, time management, and the satisfaction of earning a paycheck. Balancing school and work taught her how to manage her time effectively. She also discovered the importance of good customer service and teamwork. Earning her own money allowed her to contribute to her expenses and save for bigger goals, such as college.

After finishing high school, Dianne decided to study both arts and accounting at college. She loved creativity but also had a strong interest in numbers and finance. Combining these fields opened up many opportunities for her. She enjoyed exploring different subjects and expanding her knowledge. Studying art allowed her to express herself creatively, while accounting gave her practical skills in finance. She found that these two fields complemented each other in unexpected ways. Her understanding of finance helped her manage budgets for art projects, and her creativity made her approach to accounting more innovative.

As a teacher, Dianne found joy in helping others learn. She taught both teens and adults, sharing her knowledge in the arts and accounting. Her positive attitude and ethical approach made her popular among her students. She believes that people can keep learning throughout their lives and loves inspiring others to do so. Dianne developed engaging lessons that made complex subjects easier to understand. She used real-life examples and interactive activities to make learning fun. Seeing her students grow and succeed was the most rewarding part of her job.

Dianne has always been fascinated by new technologies. From the days of analog devices to the rise of digital technology and now artificial intelligence, she has seen many changes. She enjoys keeping up with these trends and is excited about what the future holds. She often incorporates technology into her teaching, using new tools to enhance learning, and encouraging her students to be curious and open-minded about technological advancements. Understanding technology, she believes, is important for success in today's world.

Now that she is semi-retired, Dianne enjoys a comfortable lifestyle. She still loves helping others pursue their passions. In her free time, she engages in various hobbies. She enjoys art, photography, walking, traveling, cooking, fermenting foods, playing Mahjong, tenpin bowling, and meditation. Traveling allows her to explore new places and cultures, which she finds inspiring. Cooking and fermenting foods are creative outlets that also promote health and well-being. Playing games like Mahjong and tenpin bowling keep her mind sharp and active. Meditation helps her stay focused and calm. These activities bring joy and balance to her life.

Dianne is grateful to her parents for teaching her important life lessons. They instilled in her a strong work ethic and a healthy respect for money. These values have guided her throughout her life and career. She hopes to pass on these lessons to others, especially young people who are just starting out. Learning about money management at a young age is crucial. Dianne wants to help teens develop smart money skills that will lead to financial freedom in the future. Through her teaching and writing, she aims to provide practical advice and guidance to help others achieve their goals.

Dianne continues to inspire others with her enthusiasm and dedication. Whether through teaching, mentoring, or simply sharing her experiences, she makes a positive impact on those around her. Her life reflects the values she holds dear: hard work, continuous learning, and helping others succeed. She looks forward to what the future brings and remains committed to making a difference in people's lives.

FEEDBACK & COMMENTS

Thank you for purchasing this book and I hope that you're now feeling empowered and confident about managing your personal finance.

Letting others know about your experience helps inspire Tigereye Publishing to create more great books.

Your feedback & suggestions will be much appreciated.

Simply scan the QR code below to leave your review.

Made in the USA
Monee, IL
04 November 2026

67385903R10069